BEYOND THE 4% RULE

BEYOND THE 4% RULE

The science of retirement portfolios that last a lifetime

Abraham Okusanya

MSc, CFP, AFPS, Chartered MCSI

To Funmi and Adorabelle, the centre of my universe.

ISBN-13: 978-1985721647

ISBN-10: 1985721643

First published in the United Kingdom in 2018 via CreateSpace

Copyright © 2018 Abraham Okusanya

All rights reserved. No part of this book can be reproduced without the written permission of Abraham Okusanya.

For further information please visit www.beyond4percent.com

Book Design: Sheer Design and Typesetting

Contents

Introduction: retirement reinvented 7

Annuity: the beginning of the end? 9

1. Skin in the game 16
2. The hidden dangers 43
3. What doesn't work 57
4. Safe withdrawal rate: how safe? 83
5. Busting the myth of U-shaped retirement spending 105
6. SWR 2.0: the power of flexible withdrawal strategies 115
7. Estimating probability of success 155
8. Adapting sustainable withdrawal strategies to longevity 179
9. Asset allocation and sustainable withdrawal rate 188
10. All together: baking the layer cake of sustainable withdrawal rate 215

About the author 225
Timeline, the sustainable withdrawal rate software 226
FinalytiQ 227

This project would have been impossible without my insanely brilliant team at FinalytiQ/Timelineapp.co and our incredible clients, who help us to keep the lights on.

I owe a debt of gratitude to my book designer Megan Sheer and editor Anthea Christie for knocking the book into shape with masterful finesse.

If I have seen further, it is by standing on the shoulders of giants including Bill Bengen, Michael Kitces, Prof Wade Pfau, Dr David Blanchett and others in the financial planning community, too numerous to mention.

INTRODUCTION

Retirement reinvented

'Science is a process. It's not pretending it has the right answer, it merely has the best process to get closer to that right answer.'

– Seth Godin

Retirement planning used to be so simple. Until the 1880s, most people didn't retire. People worked till they dropped. Workers – especially men – literally died with their boots on.

Then in the 1880s, the German Chancellor Otto von Bismarck presented a radical idea of financial support for older members of society. The German government created what was in effect the first retirement system: state-sponsored financial support for people over 70.

It's rumoured that von Bismarck's motive was to get rid of government opposition. But the idea caught on, not just in Germany but also in the UK and the US. And by the early 1920s, the proportion of employed men over the age of 65 had dropped significantly.

By the 1930s, many industries promised their employees some sort of pension in retirement. These were the forerunners of what's known today as defined benefit pension schemes.

But as people lived longer, the cost of providing defined benefit schemes soared out of control. It became difficult for employers to afford defined benefit pensions and individuals gradually became more responsible for saving for their old age.

Enter defined contribution schemes. Individuals simply built up savings for their old age (known as accumulation). They often had support from their employers and they got tax relief from the government.

After doing this during their working lives, most people never had to worry about how to convert their pot of money into income for the rest of their lives. There was a simple solution – an annuity!

People simply handed their pot of money to an insurance company, who offered them a guaranteed income for the rest of their lives in return.

Annuity: the beginning of the end?

'... but if you observe, people always live for ever when there is an annuity to be paid them; and she is very stout and healthy, and hardly forty. An annuity is a very serious business; it comes over and over every year, and there is no getting rid of it.'

– Jane Austen, Sense and Sensibility (1811)

Pension rules since the 1990s offered some flexibility in terms of how people drew income. Still, over 90% of people bought an annuity with their pension pot. It became the de facto retirement income product for people saving into a defined contribution pension.

Annuities were really great products. They probably still are for many people. For most of the period between 1950 and 2000, annuity rates for a 65-year-old were in double digits.

Annuities don't work in a vacuum. A retiree hands over their pension pot to an insurer in exchange for an income for a lifetime. The insurer then lends that money to the government (after taking a cut) by investing in government bonds (also known as gilts). The interest they receive from gilts is what they use to meet their obligation to the retiree.

It doesn't matter how long you live, your annuity pays an income until you die. Some annuitants will live for a long time and get more from their annuity than they paid in. Others aren't so lucky and they get a lot less. In effect, those who don't live very long subsidise those who do. Plus insurers get a tidy profit.

The financial crisis of 2008/09 marked a major turning point for the future of annuities in the UK. Like other central banks across the world, the Bank of England started money-printing programmes (also known as quantitative easing). This was an attempt to stabilise the financial system by purchasing gilts from the government.

This drove up prices on government bonds, and consequently yields were pushed to historical lows. Annuity rates took a beating.

This led to a lot of bickering between financial commentators about whether annuities were good value for money. Some experts thought yes, others thought no. Then there were those who thought people should sell the one they already had!

An increasing number of retirees developed a love-hate relationship with their annuity. Annuities became demonised, perhaps justifiably so, and this went on for some time.

Then bang! In 2014, then-Chancellor George Osborne muttered a few words in his budget speech that would change the fortunes of millions of people in retirement, for better or worse.

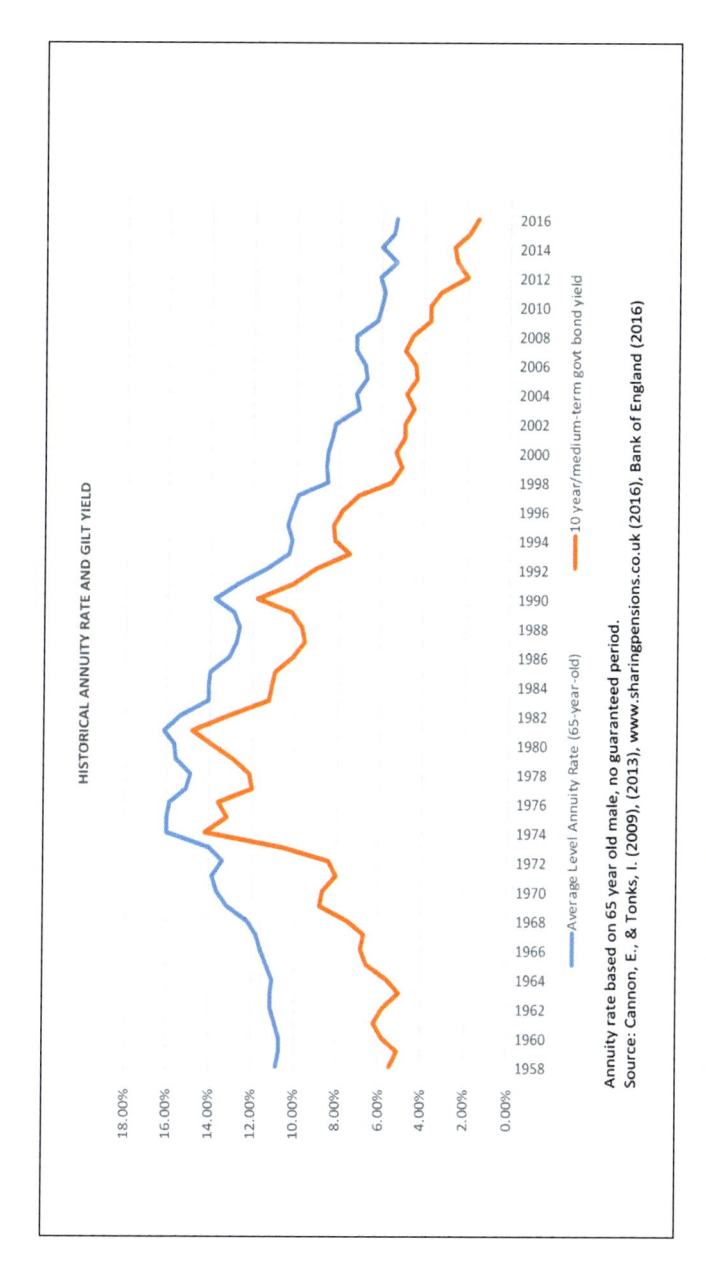

Fig. 1: Historical Annuity and UK Gilt Yield

'I am announcing today that we will legislate to remove all remaining tax restrictions on how pensioners have access to their pension pots. Pensioners will have complete freedom to draw down as much or as little of their pension pot as they want, anytime they want. No caps. No drawdown limits. Let me be clear. No one will have to buy an annuity.'

Those few seemingly harmless words essentially ended annuities as the default (real or perceived) option in retirement. In the following months, annuity rates fell to record levels. An increasing number of people are now choosing to drawdown their retirement savings without buying an annuity.

Retirees must work out how best to make their retirement income last a lifetime. This is a huge challenge and one that this book is designed to tackle.

The landscape changed for financial advisers too. For many, helping clients with retirement income planning isn't anything new. They've been doing it for donkey's years. So, you'd be forgiven for wondering why we need a new book on the topic.

But the reality is that something dramatic happened in the UK retirement planning landscape when George Osborne uttered those words.

Historically, the UK pension system had an inbuilt safety-first mechanism in its legislation and regulation. Even pension drawdown products had a safety mechanism (the GAD rates and Minimum Income Requirement) which made it hard for retired people to run out of money. But Pension Freedoms ripped up the retirement income planning rulebook and put a major dent in this inbuilt safety-first mechanism.

It's further exacerbated by falling annuity rates and the closure of increasing numbers of defined benefit schemes. An increasing number of people reaching retirement age won't have any inbuilt safety-first income beyond the State Pension. Their DC pot will be their main source of income after the State Pension.

Advisers may well have been advising on retirement income planning for some time, but they've been thrown into uncharted territory by Pension Freedoms. It's only right to question whether existing practices are still fit for purpose.

Financial advisers working in this area also carry significant risk, particularly in light of the lack of a long-stop on financial advice. They carry the potential liability for retirement income advice to their graves. Poor outcomes could see clients seeking redress from advisers. And even long after the actual client has passed on, the heirs of their estate could potentially seek redress for unsuitable advice.

What's in the book?

This book isn't designed as a substitute for a financial adviser. On the contrary, it's written with retirees and their financial advisers in mind. Both will benefit from the book.

The book explores the two fundamental schools of thought on retirement income planning – safety-first and probability-based – and how each addresses the retirement income conundrum. It's crucial to understand the strengths and the weaknesses of each. Ultimately, the question is, where do you place your trust for sustainable income in retirement? The guarantees of an insurance company or the capital markets? Is there such a thing as a middle ground?

If you trust insurer guarantees, the answer is simple. Do it the traditional way. Buy an annuity. At least to secure your basic income.

If you trust the capital markets, this book confronts the challenge of how to secure a sustainable income that lasts a lifetime from your portfolio. It delves into the details of the so-called 4% rule or, more precisely, safe withdrawal rates. This may seem to be a simple concept on the surface, but there are nuances. These include various income withdrawal strategies, asset allocation and the unavoidable question of how long before you pop your clogs.

ANNUITY: THE BEGINNING OF THE END?

This book helps retirees and their advisers navigate the treacherous retirement income landscape, using sound empirical evidence and robust, practical application. There's no trial-and-error.

I hope you enjoy reading the book as much as I've enjoyed writing it.

Happy reading.

CHAPTER 1

Skin in the game

An increasing body of research highlights the fundamental difference between retirement income planning and traditional financial planning in the accumulation stage. But I find the old fable of the chicken and the pig better illustrates this remarkable difference.

A Pig and a Chicken are walking down the road.

The Chicken says: *'Hey Pig, I was thinking we should open a restaurant!'*

Pig replies: *'Hmm, maybe, what would we call it?'*

The Chicken responds: *'How about 'ham-n-eggs'?'*

The Pig thinks for a moment and says: *'No thanks. I'd be committed, but you'd only be involved.'*

The lesson is that in a breakfast of eggs and bacon, the pig has a lot more to lose than the chicken. Retirement is the stage when an individual's pension pot transitions from a chicken into a pig. It becomes a lot more than just a number on a statement. It's what they rely on to pay their day-to-day bills, fund their lifestyle and enjoy their newly found freedom. The retiree has more skin in the game, so to speak.

Fig. 2: The chicken and the pig

Sadly, when it comes to retirement income planning, a large part of the advice profession and the financial industry continue to think like chickens, when they should think more like pigs!

We all need to understand the risks that are peculiar to this crucial stage.

Planning your retirement income strategy is one of the hardest things you'll ever do. Most people will benefit immensely from working with a financial adviser who truly understands the complexities involved. But not every financial adviser is a retirement income specialist. An emerging body of research points to the fact that retirement income planning should be considered a distinct discipline, with its own theories and practices that are based on rigorous empirical evidence.

In the medical profession, general practitioners (GPs) treat most common and non-life-threatening conditions. They play an invaluable role in caring for their patients. However, they're not allowed to cut people up. When it comes to dealing with issues relating to the intricate workings of specific organs or systems of the body, we call on specialists. After completing medical school, specialists complete additional training in a specific branch of medicine to become surgeons (of different kinds), paediatricians, obstetricians and other medical specialisms too numerous to name.

The point is that retirement income planning is a specialist branch of financial planning. And retirees should only seek to work with specialists in this area. Why? Because the problems you're trying to solve are different than during accumulation. More importantly, the consequences of misdiagnosis or mistreatment are infinitely greater. The risks, tools, theories and practices required for the job are therefore very different.

Key retirement income risks

The unique risks associated with retirement income planning sum up the distinction between the accumulation and retirement stages.

a) Diminished earning flexibility

Retirement happens at the tail end of your working life, long after earnings have peaked. Returning to work after retirement isn't a viable option for many. The practical implication is that we want to take less risk with our savings as we become more reliant on our financial assets.

b) Inflation risk

A major challenge is how to prevent inflation – the thief that keeps on taking – from depleting the buying power of your income over what may be a 30-year retirement, or possibly longer.

c) Decreasing cognitive abilities

As people get older, their ability to make a financial decision is impaired. It's estimated that financial capability declines at a rate of 1% to 2% per year from age 60[1].

---

[1] Finke M, Howe J and Huston S (2011) Old Age and the Decline in Financial Literacy, Social Science Research Network, Available at SSRN: http://ssrn.com/abstract=1948627

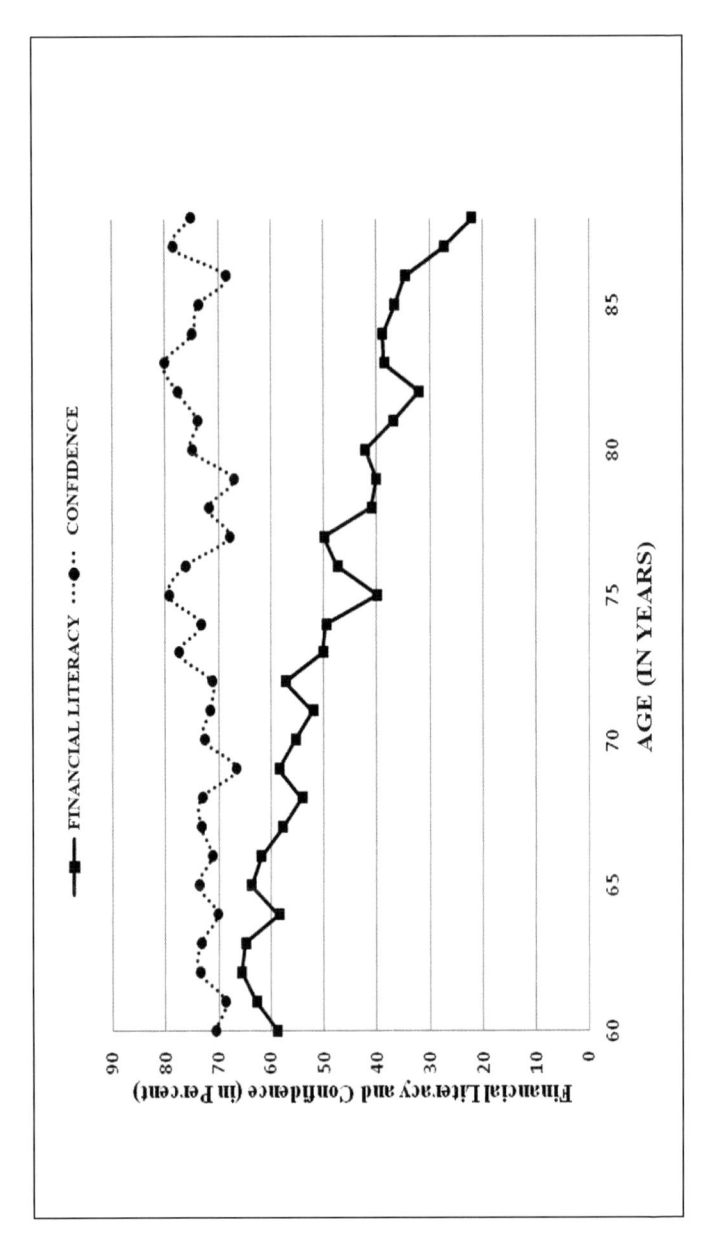

Fig. 3: Financial literacy score by age

The chart opposite shows the average self-assessed confidence with financial literacy and actual financial literacy by age from 60 to 89[2].

So, even though actual financial literacy declines with age, an individual's confidence in their own ability to make financial decisions tends to remain stable as they get older. The difference between the two is dubbed the overconfidence gap.

This makes it challenging for clients to understand the vagaries of managing a drawdown portfolio. It may even be challenging to give their adviser informed consent to manage it on their behalf.

d) Longevity risk and unknown time horizon

The fear of dying is right up there on the list of people's biggest fears. But the fear of public speaking is apparently even higher. Maybe I've got this all wrong but if that's true, then when the average person goes to a funeral, they'd rather be in the casket than do the eulogy. But I digress.

For retirees, the greatest fear shouldn't be of an untimely death, but of living too long! Indeed, research suggests that if there's anything retirees fear more than death, it's running out of money during their lifetime.

---

2 Cox, P., (2016) Helping consumers and providers manage defined contribution (DC) wealth in retirement

Retirement income planning is particularly challenging because we're planning for a finite, but precisely unknown retirement period. Without the proverbial crystal ball, it's tricky to estimate how long you're likely to live.

It's estimated that around 75% of people over age 65 live as a couple. The chance that at least one of a 65-year-old couple will live to age 100 is 24%.

So it's important to consider the survival probability for couples, not just for the individuals.

Given this long but precisely unknown time horizon, how do we make sure that a pension pot lasts a lifetime? It's a particular challenge when a retiree doesn't want to buy an annuity with all or most of their retirement savings pot.

e) Heightened sequence risk

Poor returns early in retirement can cause untold damage to your prospects of a decent income for life. Sequence risk is often confused with volatility, a traditional measure of investment risk. But it's a distinct and visible risk – particularly at the retirement income stage.

The best way to understand the impact of sequence risk on a retirement portfolio is to look at the impact of each year's return on the overall outcome for someone over a typical investment lifetime.

Suppose an individual spends 60 years invested in the capital markets. They pay into their portfolio for the first 30 years (accumulation) and they take money out for the last 30 years (decumulation).

Fig. 4 overleaf[3] shows the impact of each year of return over the entire investment period of a typical individual's lifetime. The chart quantifies the impact of each year's return and shows how much the success or failure of the overall retirement journey depends on the returns obtained in any year.

The returns in the first decade of decumulation stage (years 31 to 40 on the chart) of retirement have a disproportionate impact on the overall retirement experience. So, the order of return is as important as the level of return.

If you get good returns in the first decade of retirement, you're unlikely to run out of money, as long as you use a sensible withdrawal rate. If you get poor or even mediocre returns in the first decade of retirement, then technically speaking, you're buggered!

It has the potential to decimate the portfolio beyond repair, even if good returns happen later in retirement.

---

[3] Wade Pfau (2016), presentation slides at the FinalytiQ's Science of Retirement Conference

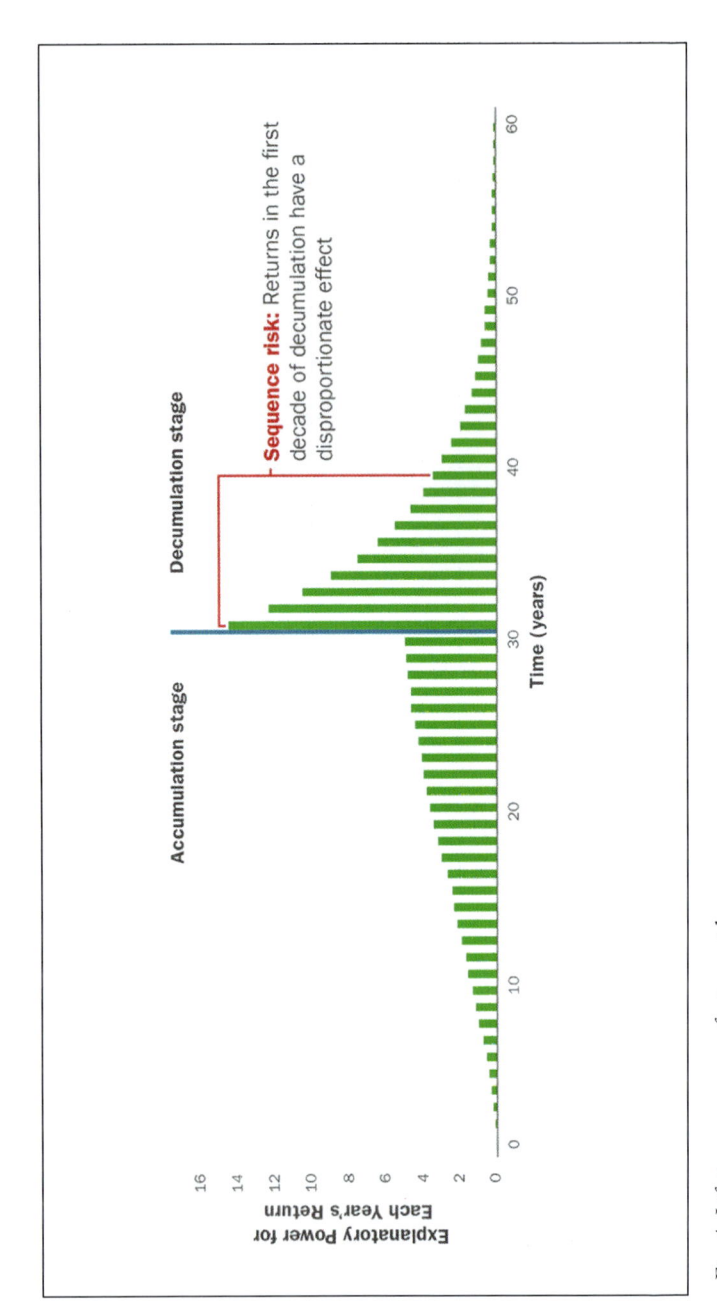

Fig. 4: Lifetime sequence of return risk

Sequence risk also exists during the accumulation stage, but it's amplified by withdrawals from a portfolio during the retirement stage.

We know that capital markets deliver good returns over the long term. But retirees taking income out of their portfolio don't have the luxury of waiting for the long term. They need income monthly or annually.

All these risks are uniquely associated with retirement income planning and we should approach them in a scientific way. It's all the more reason why retirees should strongly consider working with a financial adviser to help them.

And advice must be based on sound empirical evidence and robust, practical application as opposed to trial and error practices handed down from one adviser to another.

The yin and yang of retirement income philosophies

'The test of a first-rate intelligence is the ability to hold two opposed ideas in mind at the same time and still retain the ability to function.'

– F. Scott Fitzgerald

In Chinese philosophy, yin and yang illustrates how seemingly contrary forces may be complementary, interconnected and interdependent in the natural world. Apparently, this duality serves as the primary guidance for Chinese medicine and even martial arts.

In Western democracy, the roles of the government and opposition are well recognised. The opposition holds the government to account, and a weak opposition is generally considered bad for democracy.

It's a fact of life that every profession (and society) has its own conflicting schools of thought. Often there are two or more opposing forces that actually complement each other and are necessary to maintain balance and order.

As an emerging field of study, retirement income is no different. Retirement Income Professor Wade Pfau and Jeremy

Cooper (2014)[4] identified the two fundamental schools of thought in retirement income planning:

- safety-first
- probability-based

We can broadly classify all retirement income strategies, products and tools by using one of these two fundamentally different philosophies.

It's crucial for retirees and their advisers to understand these philosophies before they can decide the best way to meet their retirement income needs. Importantly, these different approaches embody the upsides and trade-offs involved in retirement income planning. If advisers don't fully understand these approaches, they can't communicate them effectively to clients and this could be detrimental to client outcomes.

- **The safety-first** school has its origins in the actuarial profession. It focuses on eliminating or mitigating the risk of an individual outliving their income. It asserts that retirement income planning should focus on individuals and not on historical data or group statistics. This philosophy distinguishes between essential

---

4 Pfau, Wade D. and Cooper, Jeremy, The Yin and Yang of Retirement Income Philosophies (November 10, 2014). Available at SSRN: http://ssrn.com/abstract=254811 4 or http://dx.doi.org/10.2139/ssrn.2548114

expenses to cover the cost of living and discretionary expenses for luxuries. It accepts some risks to the discretionary expenses, but the safety-first approach aims to take all risk to the essential income off the table completely.

- **The probability-based** school has its roots in the investment industry. It's about estimating the chances of running out of money in the face of market and longevity risks and planning accordingly. It's impossible to know in advance what investment returns, inflation and longevity are going to be. The probability school tests the chances of running out of money by using Monte Carlo models. The model runs thousands of possible future scenarios and estimates the probability of success or failure of a financial plan.

A retiree's retirement income strategy will be very different, depending on which approach they agree with their adviser. This is because the two schools of thought have very different answers to even the basic retirement income planning questions.

A bus ride with two retirement income eggheads

Imagine you find yourself on a long bus ride. You're sat in between two retirement income wonks – safety-first guy to your right and probability-based lady to your left. Horrified to discover who they are, your first move is to do what any sensible human being would do – find another seat!

But all the seats are taken. You accept that this is probably going to be one long, tiresome bus ride!

You decide to make the best of a bad situation. After all, you're due to retire in a couple of years, so you engage these two eggheads in a conversation on retirement income planning.

After all the usual pleasantries, you ask them your first question. Here's how the conversation might unfold...

You: *So guys, here's your chance to shine. What's the first thing I should be thinking about for my retirement income?*

Safety-first: *Prioritise essential over discretionary expenses. Essential expenses are your rice and beans – stuff you can't do without (groceries, transport, bills, etc.), so they shouldn't be subject to the vagaries of the investment markets. Discretionary expenses are things you can delay, defer or even do without completely if need be. You should plan for these but only after you've secured the essential expenses.*

Probability-based: *You're wasting your time listening to safety-first. The distinction between 'essential' and 'discretionary' expenses is a mirage. What you need is a high-level view of the total income you can reasonably live on in retirement. Most people would consider their retirement a failure if they can only meet basic needs and not their discretionary needs.*

You: *What's a reasonable amount to take from my pension pot each year so it doesn't run out?*

Safety-first: *Very simple this one. Unknown and unknowable! You should secure your essential needs first using products with guarantees, so there's no risk of running out of money.*

Probability-based: *Well, funny you should ask. I've done a lot of work on this one. Looking at historical market and inflation data over the last 100 years, even the worst case scenario would suggest that a withdrawal rate of 3% of the initial portfolio, adjusted for inflation, is a very good starting point. You might have to make some adjustments along the way, though.*

Safety-first: *Well, just because something worked in the past doesn't mean it'll work now or in the future. The future is inherently unpredictable.*

Probability-based: *Uncertainties are a part of every aspect of life, and retirement is no exception. That's why I use my Monte Carlo model to run thousands of possible scenarios. Barring a catastrophe that brings capitalism to an end, the 3% withdrawal rate should* mean you can survive some of the most severe market conditions, with small adjustments along the way.

You: *Hmmm... what's Monte Carlo? You mean the city?*

Probability-based: *Ah! the model, not the city. I use a computer to run thousands of retirement scenarios based on investment and inflation assumptions. Think of it as giving you 10,000 lives! Each of those lives represents what your retirement could look like. I must worry about the scenarios where you run out of money. I figure out what we need to do under those circumstances and we agree in advance what the plan is.*

Safety-first: *Utter nonsense! You're wasting your time. Why 10,000 lives? Why not 100,000? Or a million? Run as many scenarios as you like. Only one scenario matters to our friend here – the one they actually experience and it's unknown! Retirement funding should focus on individuals and not on the historical data or group statistics.*

You: *Hum... food for thought. How long a retirement should I plan for?*

Safety-first: *Again, unknown and unknowable. Much longer than you expect.*

Probability-based: *Looking at the Office for National Statistics cohort life expectancy table, we can estimate your survival probability to any certain age. Hang on. I've got a copy in my bag.*

(Probability-based pulls out a copy of the ONS life expectancy table)

Probability-based: *Didn't you say you turn 65 in 2020? There is a 12% chance that a 65-year-old male in 2020 will celebrate their 100th birthday. That rises to 17% for a female of the same age.*

Safety-first: *What does that mean for our friend here though? So there's a one in 10 chance of living till age 100. How does that help you plan your income? The reality is that you need an income for your lifetime. However long it is. If you say there's a 12% chance of living till a certain age and you use that as your planning horizon, what if you're wrong?*

It's getting a bit heated, so you butt in...

You: *Calm down guys, no need to throw punches...*

Safety-first: *Sorry. It drives me nuts when people talk about retirement income planning in terms of probability. All these statistics and probability based on the whole population have very little meaning for ordinary people. My method works based on every individual's circumstances, regardless of market conditions.*

You: *Final question guys. When it comes to ensuring decent reliable income in retirement, where should an individual really place their trust?*

Safety-first: *The contractual guarantee of insurance is your best bet for your essential spending.*

Probability-based: *I'll take my chances with the capital markets, thank you very much. It's the bedrock of capitalism.*

A BUS RIDE WITH TWO RETIREMENT INCOME EGGHEADS

Bus driver announces over the speaker: *Ladies and gentlemen, we have reached our destination! Thank you very much for riding with us and have a great day.*

You give a sigh of relief and quickly grab your coat. You try to say goodbye and thanks to the retirement eggheads, but they don't notice you. They're still having a heated debate about what's best for you!

The table overleaf provides a key summary of the different tools, techniques, and strategies employed by each school of thought.

Table 1: Summary of probability-based vs. safety-first

	Probability-based	Safety-first
Budget	High level	Detailed Budget
Modelling tool	• Historical or Monte Carlo model • Withdrawal policy statement	• Cash flow plan • Funding priority (essential-vs-discretionary)
Longevity risk	Managed using survival probability	Hedged using contractual guarantees
Withdrawal strategy	Systematic/rules-based withdrawal strategies	Liability-matching based on a hierarchy of income needs
Tradeoff	Can adjust income down at some point during retirement to avoid running out in severe market conditions	Prioritise income needs. Retirees may sacrifice some lifestyle and legacy goals to secure their essential income
Upside	• Flexibility • Higher income and legacy if market turns out to be favourable	Essential income not subject to vagaries of the market
Retirement income product	• Diversified investment portfolios	• Annuity for essential spending • Investment-linked annuity • Diversified portfolios only used for discretionary spending
Risk profile	Medium to high	Low to medium
Flexibility to income adjustment	Medium to high	Low to medium
Maintenance	High	Low
Difficulty	Complex	Simple

Modern Portfolio Theory vs. Modern Retirement Theory

The empirical foundation for the probability-based school is the seminal paper published in the Journal of Financial Planning in 1994[5] by engineer-turned-financial planner, William Bengen. A key aspect of Bengen's work is the idea of optimal asset allocation for a retirement portfolio. This draws on the Modern Portfolio Theory, pioneered by Harry Markowitz in 1952. It explores how a portfolio of multiple assets maximises returns for a given level of risk.

The safety-first school has its empirical basis in lifecycle finance, put forward by Zvi Bodie[6]. The premise is that, given the uncertainties of returns, inflation and life expectancy, retirees should allocate their resource in a way that optimises lifetime consumption (ie income needs). The focus shouldn't be just portfolio returns and total wealth.

---

5 Bengen, William P (1994) 'Determining Withdrawal Rates Using Historical Data'. Journal of Financial Planning 7, 4 (October): 171–180

6 Bodie, Zvi and Treussard, Jonathan and Willen, Paul, The Theory of Life-Cycle Saving and Investing (May 2007). FRB of Boston Public Policy Discussion Paper No. 07-3. Available at SSRN: http://ssrn.com/abstract=1002388 or http://dx.doi.org/10.2139/ssrn.1002388

Hierarchy of retirement income needs

One of the best applications of the safety-first school is the Modern Retirement Theory (MRT). This was put forward by financial planner Jason Branning and academic Ray Grubbs in their 2010 paper published in the Journal of Financial Planning[7].

The premise is that there are differences between institutional and personal finance, so Modern Portfolio Theory can be misapplied to individual clients. Rather than constructing a retirement income strategy that's dependent on the performance of a portfolio, every retiree must confront the issues of their unknown future health and longevity. MRT recognises that future events are always unique to individuals and retirement income strategy should not be based on historical data or group statistics.

The central point is that because the future is unknown, retirees should seek to prioritise their spending/income needs. They should use guaranteed sources of income to secure essential expenses first. Only then should they consider using a volatile portfolio to fund discretionary expenses. The theory introduces a hierarchy of retirement income needs.

This creates a framework and order for meeting a client's retirement objectives and income needs.

---

7 Branning, Jason K, and M Ray Grubbs (2010) 'Using a Hierarchy of Funds to Reach Client Goals'. Journal of Financial Planning 23, 12 (December): 31–33.

Fig. 5: The hierarchy of retirement income needs in the safety-first philosophy. Source: Branning, Jason K, and M Ray Grubbs (2010)

- Essential income that's stable, secure and lasts a lifetime. This mustn't be subject to the vagaries of the investment market. This would include the State Pension, defined benefit pensions, annuities and income from inflation-hedged gilts.

- Contingency funds that are easily accessible, eg cash account.

- Discretionary funds to meet lifestyle expenses. This is only funded after the essential income and contingency fund needs have been met. Possible sources of income are a drawdown pot, Individual Savings Account (ISA) and other investments.

- Legacy funds for a retiree who wants to pass on some of their wealth to their beneficiaries. This should only be addressed after the first three needs.

The key strength of the MRT is its simplicity. It's low-maintenance, robust and it mitigates risk. It's relatively easy for advisers to implement and for clients to understand. More importantly, it works regardless of the market conditions. Many clients may have to give up on leaving a legacy in order to secure essential and discretionary income. This trade-off is built into the framework.

As you can see, each school of thought has its own strengths and weakness that advisers should fully understand.

Sustainable withdrawal rates

Bengen's central accomplishment was to establish a safe withdrawal rate (SWR) from a simple equity-bond portfolio. He used actual historical market data, as opposed to average return. The SWR is the highest withdrawal rate, as a percentage of the initial portfolio, adjusted for inflation each year that someone can use without depleting the portfolio. That's over any 30-year retirement period in history. It's based on the worst sequence of market return and inflation over the last 100 years. Adapting this same framework for the UK, Professor Wade Pfau established that the SWR for the UK is 3.05%, based on a 50/50 equity-bond portfolio.

The main weakness of Bengen's SWR is the assumption that a retiree will maintain the same level of real spending during their retirement. This makes budgeting more predictable, but it implies that a retiree will play a game of chicken with their portfolio. They'll increase their withdrawal with inflation every single year, while their portfolio plummets to zero. For most people, real spending actually falls in retirement, albeit gradually. According to research by the International Longevity Centre, as people get older, they spend progressively less on consumption, regardless of their income. A household headed by someone aged 80 spends 43% less, on average, than a household headed by a 50-year-old[8]. We'll come back to the subject of flexible withdrawal strategies.

It's best to think of these schools of thought as two radically different ends of a spectrum.

Every retirement income product strategy will sit somewhere in between the two extremes as shown below.

Annuities and other retirement income products with contractual guarantees sit at the safety-first end of the spectrum. Drawdown, managed using safe withdrawal rate strategies, sits at the other end in the probability-based camp.

There's a range of products and strategies sitting in between – some with features of both schools. A small number of hybrid or blended retirement income products are available in the market, designed to give clients the best of both worlds. This is achieved by combining two or more products, (eg annuities) to provide essential income and drawdown for discretionary income.

---

8   Brancati C, Beach B, Franklin B and Jones M (2015): Understanding retirement journeys: Expectations vs reality. International Longevity Centre. November, 2015. Available online at http://www.ilcuk.org.uk/index.php/publications/publication_details/understanding_retirement_journeys_expectations_vs_reality

Decisions, Decisions

Now you understand the two main retirement income philosophies, which one chimes with you the most?

Do you trust the guarantee of an insurance company or will you take your chances with the capital markets?

Clearly, several factors play a role in the suitability of a retirement income strategy. It's impossible to include all the factors likely to influence retirement income strategy in a book. One of the advantages of working with an adviser is that they will help you create a strategy for your unique situation.

The probability-based approach is likely to be uncomfortable for retirees if they have a smaller pension pot, low-to-medium risk profile and insufficient guaranteed income to meet their basic needs. Also, if you need more than 3% of the initial portfolio to meet your ongoing income and you have few other assets to fall back on if your portfolio runs out, a safety-first approach could be more appropriate.

Given the high-maintenance nature of the probability-based approach, it's likely that the ongoing cost involved (for the platform, funds, and advice) defeats any likely benefit to the client.

You may feel more comfortable with a safety-first approach if you've got a low risk appetite and are likely to wake up in a cold sweat worrying about your portfolio.

In this case, the answer is straightforward – consider securing your baseline income through an annuity. And then if you still have any liquid funds left, consider pension drawdown for the rest (see Fig. 5: The hierarchy of retirement income needs in the safety-first philosophy). You can skip the rest of the book – unless of course, curiosity won't let you.

If the probability-based approach appeals, then you've a big job on your hands. How do you work out the sustainable withdrawal rate for your pension? What about asset allocation and charges? And for God's sake, how do you work out how long you're likely to live for?

We address these questions in the rest of this book. We delve into the all the nuances around meeting retirement income needs with the probability-based philosophy. This includes an in-depth discussion of safe withdrawal strategies and the associated risks.

CHAPTER 2

The hidden dangers

What's the world's deadliest animal to humans? Most people think of beasts with large teeth and fearsome reputations, such as the lion, rhino, wolf or the oft-cited hippo.

It's actually the tiny mosquito that does the most damage. It causes more deaths than virtually any other animal: responsible for about 725,000 human deaths annually. Only human beings themselves come close, with a tally of about 425,000. And what of man's supposed best friend? Dogs kill about 25,000 people each year, almost exclusively because of rabies.

Now compare these figures to those recorded for the so-called most dangerous animals: wolf (10), lion (100) or hippo (500). These fearsome beasts don't even appear in the top 10 deadliest animals.

So, what's all this got to do with retirement income planning?

It's a classic example of our tendency as humans to misunderstand risk. It's particularly relevant when you think about portfolio risk. When the new Pension Freedoms were announced by Chancellor George Osborne in 2014, many commentators

The World's Deadliest Animals
Number of people killed by animals per year

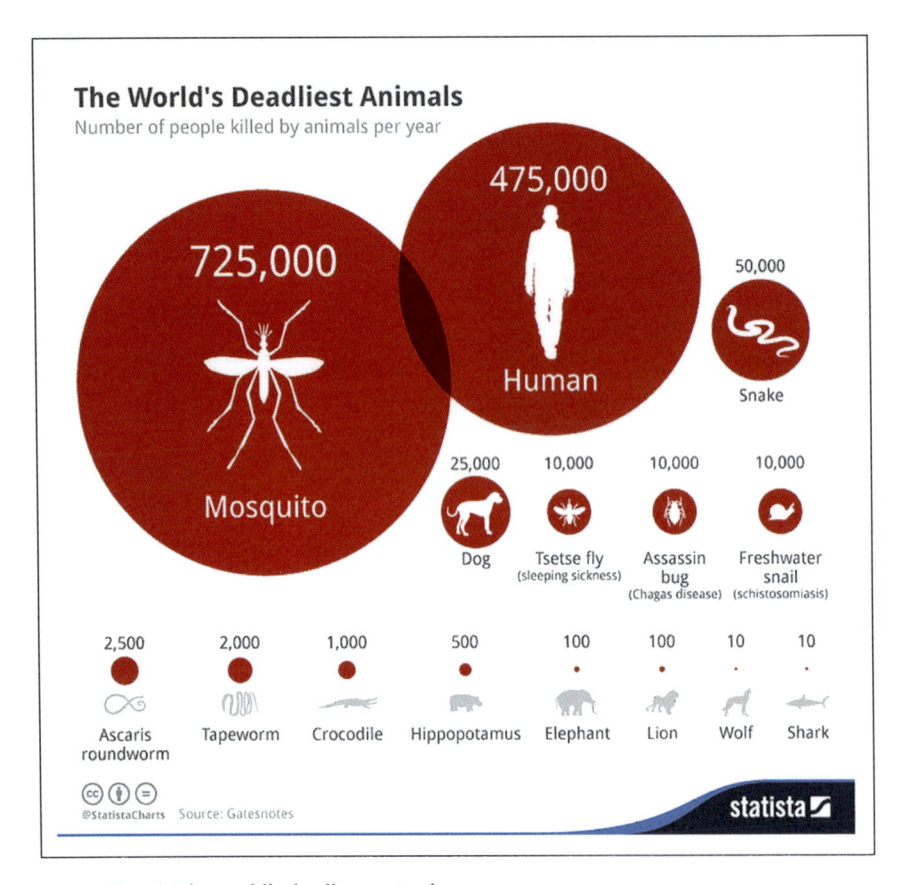

- Mosquito: 725,000
- Human: 475,000
- Snake: 50,000
- Dog: 25,000
- Tsetse fly (sleeping sickness): 10,000
- Assassin bug (Chagas disease): 10,000
- Freshwater snail (schistosomiasis): 10,000
- Ascaris roundworm: 2,500
- Tapeworm: 2,000
- Crocodile: 1,000
- Hippopotamus: 500
- Elephant: 100
- Lion: 100
- Wolf: 10
- Shark: 10

@StatistaCharts Source: Gatesnotes statista

Fig. 6: The world's deadliest animals

focused on the risk that people could squander their savings on Lamborghinis and cruises. Other widely publicised risks include pensioners being scammed, or lured into questionable investments, be it car park schemes in China or forestry investments in Brazil.

The real risks for most retirees are more subtle. As more people go into drawdown, the real risk is that most investors don't pay enough attention to that most silent of portfolio killers: the negative sequence of return. Clients risk being blindsided by these silent dangers while they worry about the more obvious risks, such as major market crashes. These subtle dangers are particularly relevant to retirement portfolios. This is because withdrawals amplify market risk in a way that's obscured by the use of time-weighted returns and the averaging of long-term returns. So, many advisers and clients don't notice until it's too late.

Historical evidence of sequence risk and why it matters in retirement income planning

Sequence risk is perhaps the most significant risk to maintaining a lifetime income for people following a probability-based retirement income approach.

When I think of sequence risk, I think of the words of the legendary Eric Morecambe, *'I'm playing all the right notes, but not necessarily in the right order.'*

Sequence risk is the risk that the *order* of investment returns is going to be unfavourable. This risk exists at accumulation stage, but it's amplified by withdrawals from a portfolio during the retirement stage. If you get good returns in the early part of retirement, you're unlikely to run out of money with a sensible withdrawal rate of say 4% or even 5%. If you get poor or even mediocre returns in the early part of retirement, the technical term is, as I've said, *'buggered!'*

I also call sequence risk 'pound-cost ravaging'. Returns in the early period of retirement have a disproportionate effect on the overall outcome, regardless of long-term returns over the entire retirement period. And if it's not properly managed, pound-cost ravaging can cause untold havoc.

To illustrate this, let's look at evidence from actual historical data over the 117 years, between 1900 and 2016, using the Dimson, Marsh and Stratton Global Investment Returns Database.

In this research, we need to explore the relationship between historical sustainable withdrawal over a 30-year period and real returns over each of the three decades of retirement within that 30-year period. For this purpose, sustainable withdrawal rate is the percentage of the initial portfolio you could take from a portfolio and subsequently adjust for inflation, without running out of money over 30 years.

So, for a £100,000 portfolio, a withdrawal rate of 4% gives you an annual income of £4,000 in the first year. The £4,000 is then adjusted for inflation every single year over 30 years, regardless of portfolio size during those subsequent years. The withdrawal rate is expressed as a percentage of the portfolio balance **only** in the first year of retirement.

The Test

- I've expressed the sustainable withdrawal in monetary terms (rather than percentages) using the term sustainable income, based on a £100,000 portfolio. The sustainable income is the maximum annual inflation-adjusted income you can take if you want to run down the portfolio balances to zero at the end of 30 years.

- For this, I looked at every 30-year period between 1900 and 2016, inclusive. So, the first 30-year period runs between 1900-1929, then 1901-1930, 1902-1931... and the final 30-year period runs between 1986-2016. This gives 87 scenarios.

- The portfolio is composed of 50% UK equities and 50% UK bonds, rebalanced annually.

- I've not applied a fee because the point is to examine the relationship between returns and sustainable withdrawals. But when I re-tested with fees applied, the findings were the same.

- Finally, I examined the average real return in the first, second and third decades of each 30-year retirement period.

The Result

Fig. 7 opposite shows the annual sustainable income (inflation-adjusted) against the average real return in the first decade of retirement.

In Fig. 7 you see a very strong correlation between return in the first decade and the sustainable income for the overall 30-year period. But look at the next chart. It shows the annual sustainable income (inflation-adjusted) against the average real return in the second and third decades of retirement.

As you can see in Fig. 8, the relationship between the sustainable income over a 30-year period and the return in the second and third decade isn't all that strong.

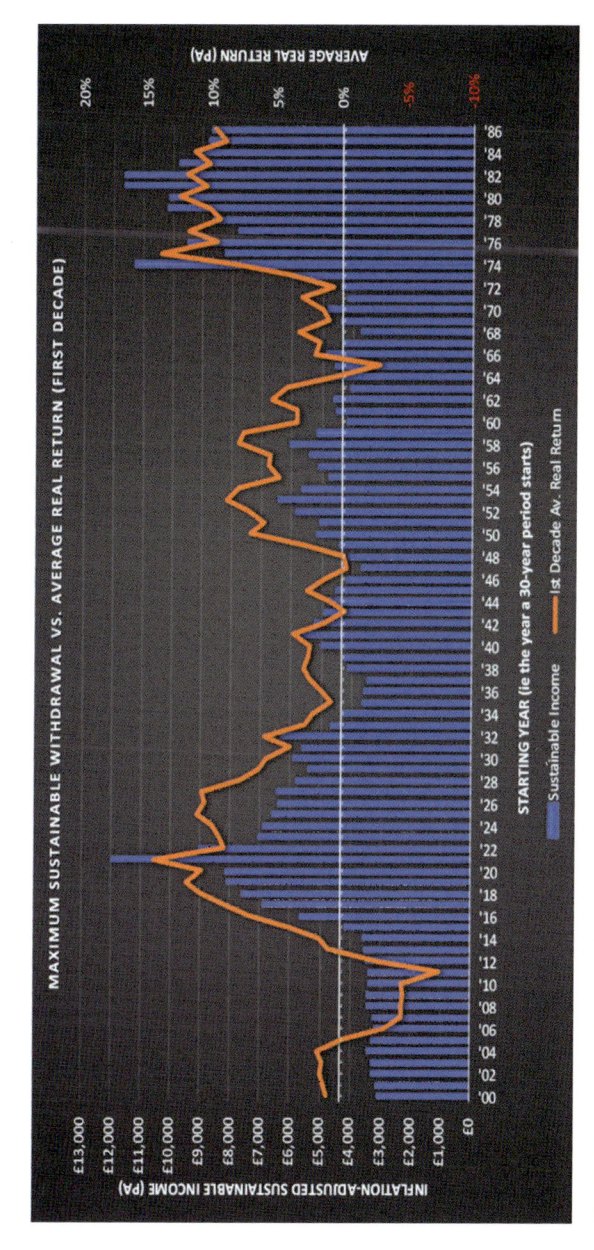

Fig. 7: Sustainable withdrawal vs. average real return in the first decade

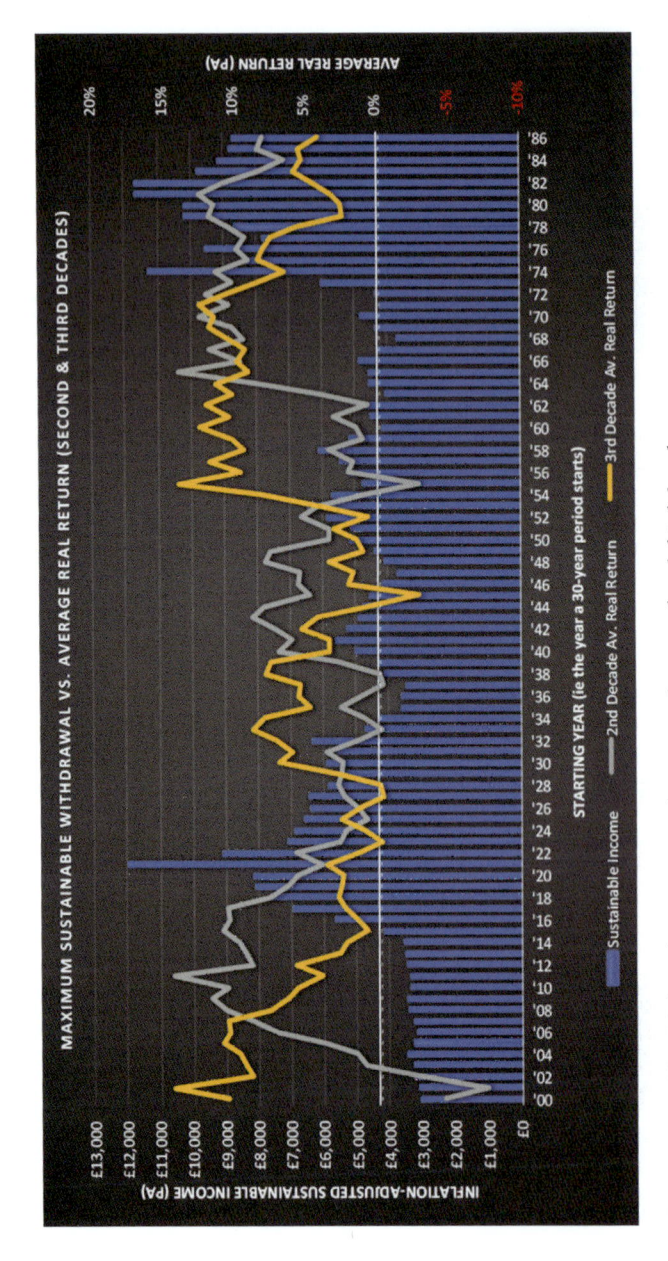

Fig. 8: Sustainable withdrawal vs. average real return in the second and third decades

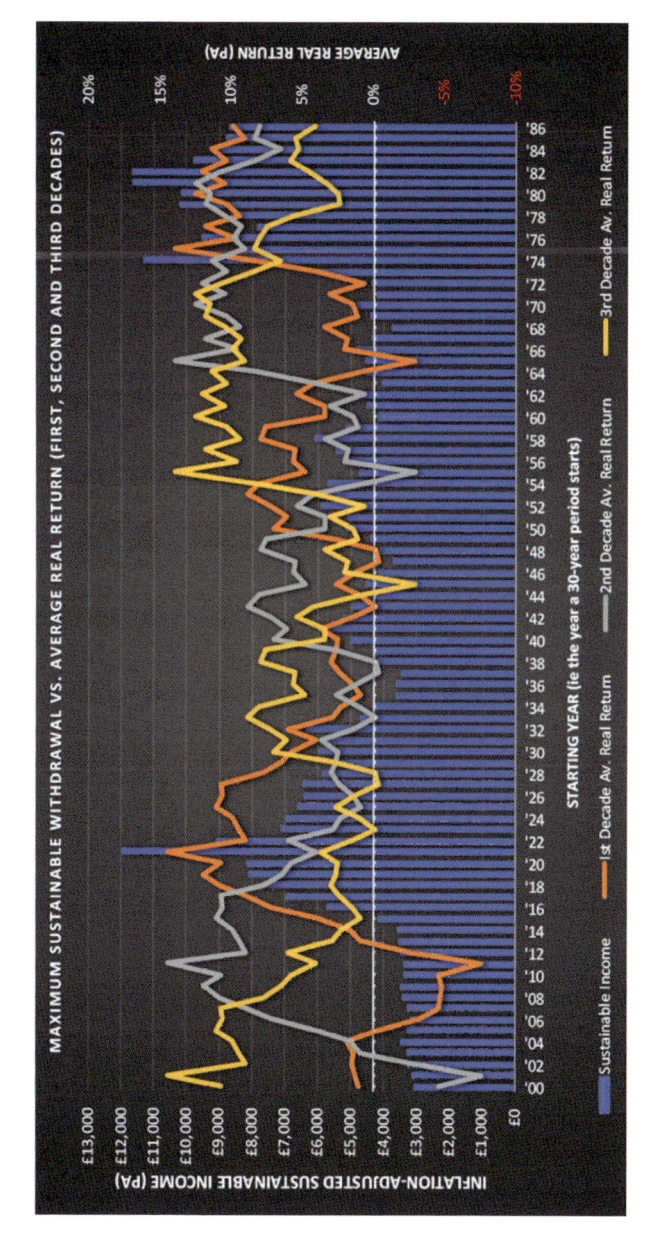

Fig. 9: Sustainable withdrawal vs. average real return in the first, second and third decades

Fig. 9 is the earlier two charts combined. It shows the annual sustainable income (inflation-adjusted) against the average real return in the first, second and third decades of retirement.

This result shows a strong correlation between sustainable income over any 30-year period and the average real return in the first decade of retirement. In years where the average real return for the first decade of retirement is high, the sustainable income over the 30-year period tends to be high, and vice versa.

Take, for example, a 30-year period starting in 1921. The average real return in the first decade was nearly 14.4%, compared to 3.9%pa in the second decade and 3.6% in the third decade of retirement. Someone starting their retirement in 1921 could have enjoyed an annual income of £12,000, adjusted for inflation over the subsequent 30 years. (A whopping withdrawal rate of 12%!) Why? Because they had a great first decade. The return in the second and third decades didn't matter as much.

Take another example: a 30-year period starting in 1969. The average real return in the first decade was a meagre 1.44%, compared to 10.2% in the second decade and 11.7% in the third. Never mind fabulous double-digit returns in the second and third decades of retirement, the sustainable income over the 30-year period was no more than £4,533pa (or a withdrawal rate of 4.5%).

Correlation between sustainable income and return	Real return	Nominal return
1st decade of retirement	83.0%	66.0%
2nd decade of retirement	26.4%	14.0%
3rd decade of retirement	-33.2.%	-25.9%
30-year average	65.1%	26.2%

Fig. 10: Correlation between sustainable income and return

Fig. 10 shows the correlation between average real return in each decade of a 30-year retirement and the sustainable withdrawal over the entire period.

Fig. 10 shows an 83% positive correlation between the sustainable withdrawal rate over a 30-year period and the real returns in the first decade of retirement! This compares to a 26% correlation between sustainable income and average real return in the second decade and a correlation of – 33.2% (a negative correlation) to the average real return in the third decade of retirement.

Coefficient of determination

We can explore the relationship between withdrawal rates and returns a little further. This time, we look at the coefficient of determination (R squared) between return in each decade of retirement and the sustainable withdrawal rates for the entire 30-year period.

R squared, or R^2 is a number that indicates the proportion of the differences in the dependent variable that is predictable from the independent variable(s).

In this case, we want to explore how much the differences in sustainable withdrawal rates can be explained or predicted by returns in the first, second and third decade of a 30-year retirement.

As Fig. 11 below shows, 69% of the differences in sustainable withdrawal rate can be explained or predicted by the inflation-adjusted return in the first decade of a 30-year retirement. Returns in the second and third decades only explained 7% and 11%, respectively. The average return over the entire 30 years only explained 42% of the variability in sustainable withdrawal rates over the same 30-year period.

The conclusion?

Return in the first decade of retirement is the main driver of sustainable income over the entire 30-year period. And the way you draw income from your retirement portfolio needs to be carefully managed, particularly in the early part of retirement.

Sequence risk is no bogeyman. Empirical data shows that it does exist. It's vile and dangerous.

Sequence risk is the primary reason someone drawing income from their portfolio is likely to run out of money, even at a modest withdrawal rate of 4% or 5%.

The question is not whether capital markets will deliver a decent average return over your retirement period. It's

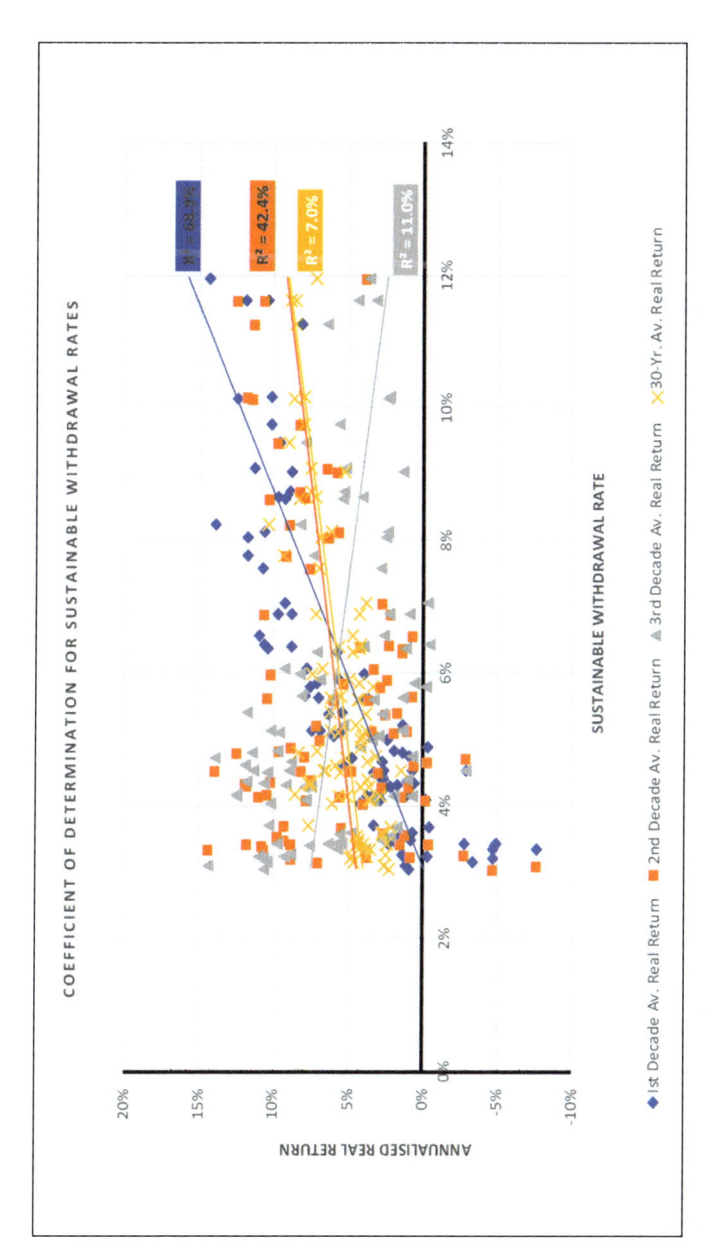

Fig. 11: Coefficient of determination for sustainable withdrawal rates.

whether the returns will come when you need them most – in the early part of your retirement.

Accordingly, it's crucial to understand and manage the havoc sequence risk can cause to a retirement plan.

Other than longevity risk, I can't think of any other retirement risk that's as potent as sequence risk. In fact, if a retiree gets a good sequence of return, longevity risk won't be an issue for most people. Yes, that's a bold statement, but one I can't emphasise enough.

It's important that we use the right tools to model sequence risk. Traditional deterministic tools do a terrible job of this. A cash flow model assuming a net return of 3%pa will show that a withdrawal rate of 5% inflation-adjusted is sustainable over a 30-year period. In reality, that plan would have failed in over 50% of actual historical scenarios.

We need to prepare clients for the possibility that they might experience a poor sequence of return in retirement. We need to have an action plan if that happens. And, we need to understand the withdrawal strategies that can mitigate sequence risk.

This is a good thing. In a sense, sequence risk is a blessing in disguise; since the early part of retirement has so much impact on the overall outcome, we can put together a framework and help clients manage this stage. We can do it with confidence that the later part of retirement will be a little less stressful.

CHAPTER 3

What doesn't work

Before we delve into how best to manage the key challenges in retirement income planning, I want to explore several common practices and why they fail woefully to address the problem. In fact, some of these approaches may well be downright harmful.

It ain't volatility, stupid!

The movie *The Big Short* opens with the quote...

'It ain't what you don't know that gets you into trouble. It's what you know for sure that just ain't so.' – Mark Twain

The quote sums up the dangers of thinking you know something that isn't actually true. There's only one problem: Mark Twain probably didn't say it. Oh, the irony.

In a misguided attempt to manage sequence risk in retirement income portfolios, a great deal of effort is devoted to managing volatility. This has resulted in a vast number of volatility-managed funds and model portfolios, peddled by asset managers to advisers and clients in retirement.

The trouble is, managing volatility in a retirement portfolio is, for the most part, a red herring. It's a bit like bringing a knife to a gun fight.

In a retirement income portfolio, sequence risk is your enemy. Not volatility. Sequence risk is often confused with volatility within the financial industry. I fell into the same trap in my early days of researching retirement income strategies. But now I've looked at the empirical data more closely, I realise that the two are related, but they're different.

Volatility is the day-to-day movement in your portfolio. It's measured using standard deviation – the amount your portfolio return deviates from the average over any given time period.

Sequence risk on the other hand relates to the order of portfolio returns.

Volatility has very little impact on the order of returns. Two portfolios might have the same average return (mean) and volatility (standard deviation) over a given period of time. But if the **order** (sequence) of returns is different, then the sustainable income will be different.

Got it? OK.

The Test

There's an over 80% correlation between returns in the early part of retirement and the sustainable withdrawal rate over a 30-year retirement period. But, I find little correlation between volatility – the industry de facto measure of risk – and sustainable income.

It doesn't matter what period you look at. Income is as likely to be high and sustainable with a high-volatility portfolio as it is with a low-volatility portfolio.

Correlation between sustainable income and return/volatility	Real return	Nominal return	Volatility
1st decade of retirement	83.0%	66.0%	8.2%
2nd decade of retirement	26.4%	14.0%	-6.8%
3rd decade of retirement	-33.2%	-25.9%	-38.8%
30-year average	65.1%	26.2%	32.0%

Fig. 12: Correlation between sustainable income and return/volatility

There's less than a 10% correlation between volatility in the first decade of retirement and the sustainable income over a 30-year period. And I only found a 32% correlation over the entire 30-year period.

Sustainable withdrawal rate has little to do with volatility.

Coefficient of determination

Just as we did with returns, we can explore the relationship between volatility and sustainable withdrawal rate by looking at the coefficient of determination (R squared) between the two.

Again, the sustainable withdrawal rate is the dependent variable. And R squared tells us how much of the difference in sustainable withdrawal rates is explained or predicted by volatility.

The result shows that volatility over the first, second and third decades of retirement explains less than 2% of variability in sustainable withdrawal rate. Indeed, the average volatility over the entire 30-year period only explained around 15% of differences in sustainable withdrawal rates.

My findings are consistent with Kenigsberg[9] et al. (2014) who noted: *'To further test whether sequence of return (SOR) risk in the first decade overshadows volatility risk in determining the maximum Sustainable Withdrawal Rate (SWR), we ran a*

---

9   Kenigsberg M, Mazumdar P and Feinschreiber S (2014): Return Sequence and Volatility: Their Impact on Sustainable Withdrawal Rates. The Journal of Retirement 2014; 2: 81.

regression analysis on historical maximum SWR (as a dependent variable) first with the first decade's real return and then with the first decade's volatility as possible independent variables, using a 50/40/10 portfolio and the historical returns for the 702 complete 30-year periods between January 1926 and May 2014. We found that using the first decade's real return as the independent variable produces an R2 value of 73%, whereas the regression using the first decade's volatility yields an R2 of only 1%. Although the use of overlapping periods may complicate this statistical approach, we think the analysis at least suggests a greater influence from sequence than from volatility.'

Investors may be tempted to use investment strategies designed to produce relatively low volatility (and accept the typically lower returns that come with them) during the early part of their retirements in order to minimise the probability of an adverse sequence of returns. But this is not necessarily effective. A strategy that produces low volatility may nonetheless deliver a highly disadvantageous sequence of returns because SOR risk and volatility, although not unrelated, are not the same thing. A poor SOR can just as easily be the product of persistence in returns (or autocorrelation) as of volatility.

A tale of two sisters

Take two sisters: Mrs Unlucky, who started her retirement in 1906, and her much younger sister, Mrs Lucky, who started her retirement in 1924. They both invested in a portfolio comprising 50% UK equities and 50% UK bonds.

	Mrs Unlucky (1906)	Mrs Lucky (1924)
30yr. nominal return (%pa)	5.72%	5.73%
30yr. volatility (%pa)	10.41%	10.46%
30yr. real return (%pa)	4.75%	4.33%
1st decade real return (%pa)	-3.28%	9.82%
2nd decade real return (%pa)	7.04%	2.22%
3rd decade real return (%pa)	10.48%	0.95%

Fig. 13: Mrs Lucky Vs. Mrs Unlucky

Over the subsequent 30-year period, they both enjoyed good average return of 5.7%pa (nominal) and very similar levels of volatility (about 10.4%) in their portfolio. Their real returns were also very similar, at over 4%pa. But in terms of sustainable income from their portfolios? It's night and day! For some strange reason, Mrs Lucky's portfolio would have supported twice that of her sister over a period of 30 years.

Fig. 14 shows what would have happened if they both took no income from their £100,000 portfolio over the subsequent 30-year period.

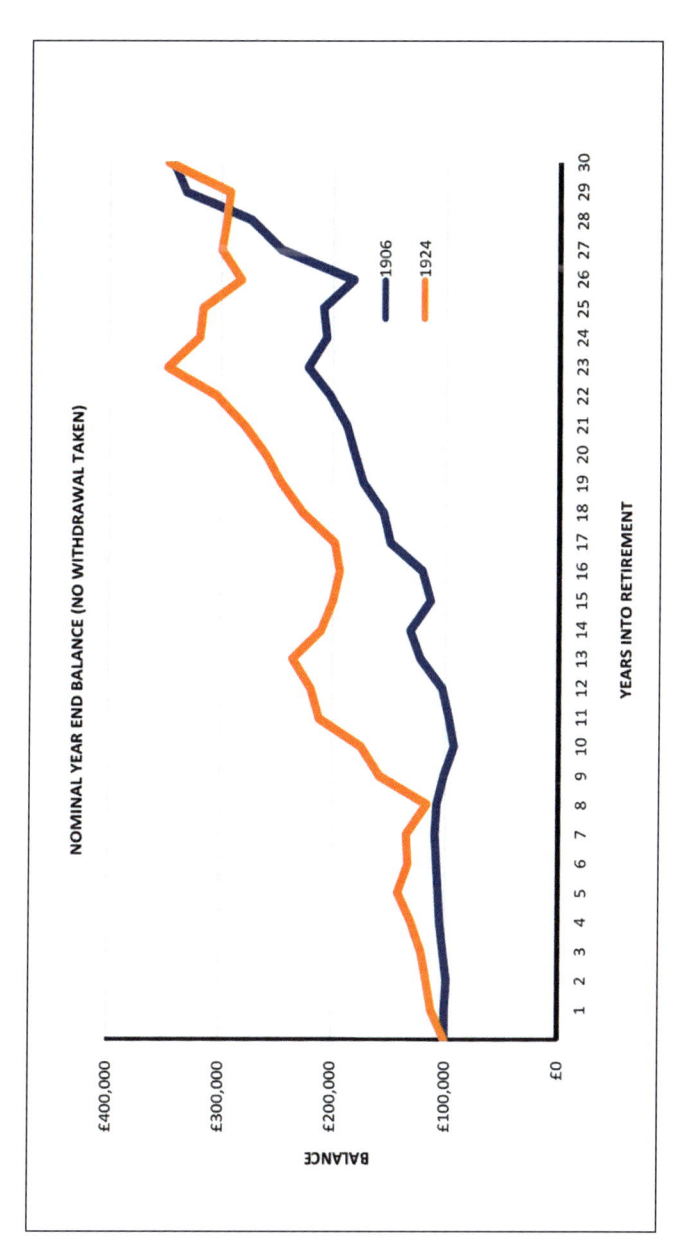

Fig. 14: Year-end portfolio balance over 30 years with no withdrawal

But suppose they both took an income of £5,000pa from their portfolios, without adjusting for inflation over a 30-year period? As Fig. 15 shows, Mrs Unlucky (1906) ran out of money while Mrs Lucky (1926) ended up with more than £100,000!

How could that be? Same average returns. Same volatility. But very different income from their portfolios.

It's very simple: Mrs Unlucky got stitched up by sequence risk. The order of return was unfavourable.

In the first decade, Mrs Unlucky got a return of -3.28%pa compared to Mrs Lucky's 9.82%pa. And it didn't matter that Mrs Unlucky's portfolio gave a decent return of 7.04%pa and 10.48%pa in the second and third decades of her retirement. The damage had already been done.

So what?

Sequence risk is the primary investment risk in retirement. Not volatility.

From a portfolio point of view, many asset managers are barking up the wrong tree. Volatility-managed solutions designed for retirement income most likely won't work. In fact, taking volatility off the table may end up being dangerous. Add in the impact of high fees that these products typically charge, and they may amplify the dangers of sequence risk rather than reduce it.

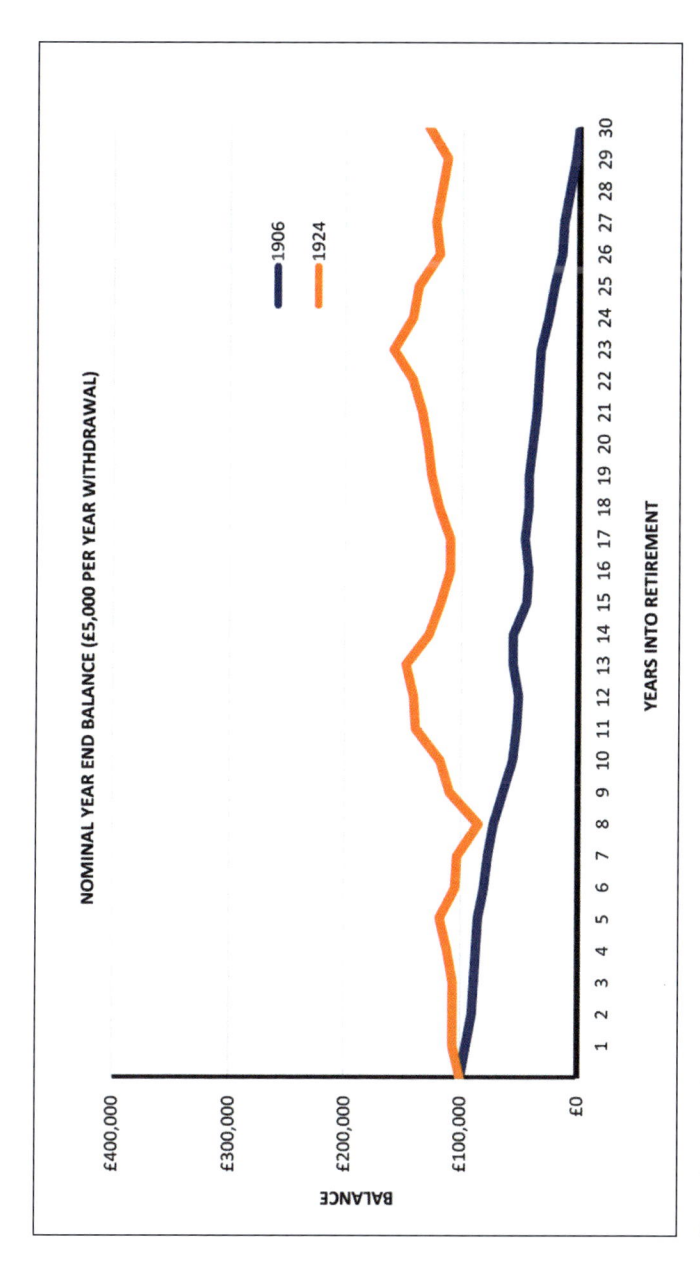

Fig. 15: Year-end portfolio balance over 30 years with £5,000pa withdrawal

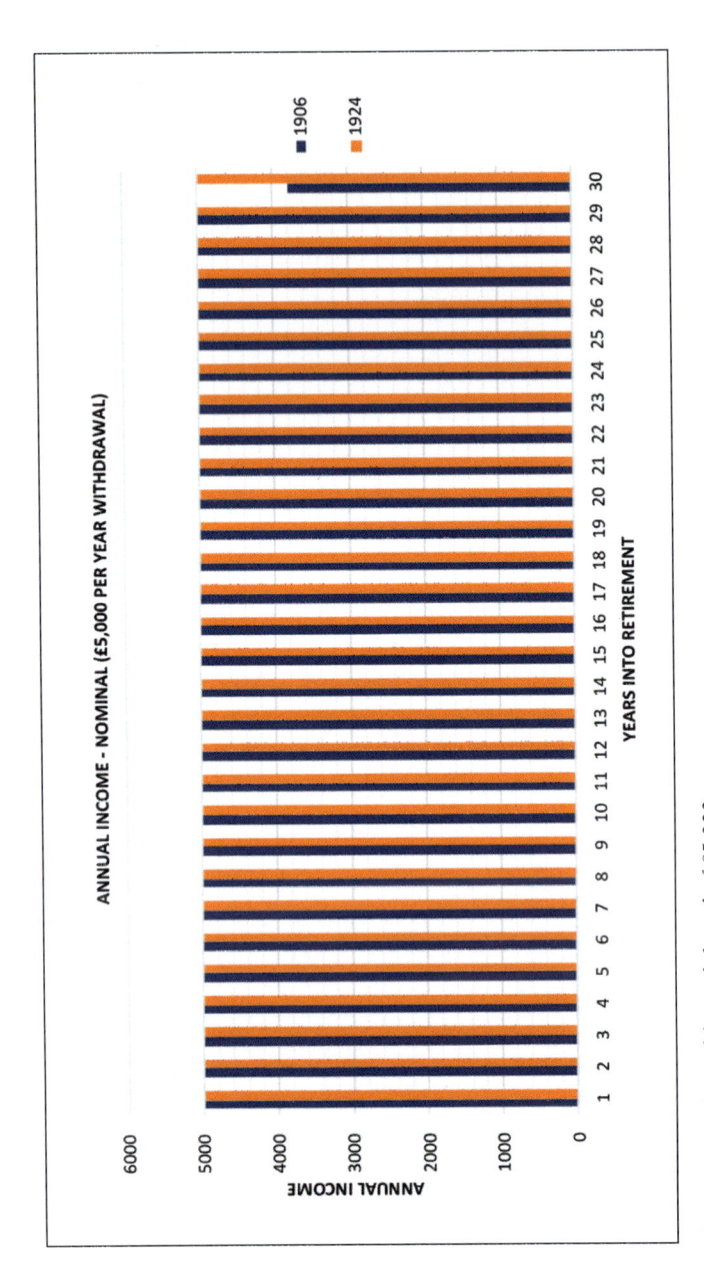

Fig. 16: Annual portfolio withdrawal of £5,000

Controlling volatility doesn't necessarily control sequence risk. This is because sequence risk is exacerbated by withdrawals from a portfolio, not by volatility.

Natural yield: a totally bonkers retirement income strategy

I'm often asked, how realistic is it to rely on natural yield to meet retirement income needs?

The rationale is that by relying on the natural yield from their portfolio, retirees can avoid drawing on their capital or selling fund units, so they avoid the dangers of sequence risk.

The natural yield approach contrasts with the total return approach. The total return approach seeks to draw income from capital growth and dividends in a sustainable way.

Some asset managers promise stable natural yield to retirees. So, it's no surprise that the consumer financial press is awash with articles on this approach. One by my friend Sam Brodbeck in the Telegraph[10] sums up the approach rather nicely: *'The idea is to ignore the fluctuating capital value of a portfolio and only take the natural yield. An original £100,000 investment might dip to £80,000 or rise to £120,000 in terms of value, but investors should resist the urge to touch the capital.'*

The trouble is, this approach is bonkers for several reasons.

---

[10] Sam Brodbeck (October, 2016) 'Can I live off the natural yield of my portfolio?' http://www.telegraph.co.uk/investing/funds/can-i-live-off-the-natural-yield-of-my-portfolio/

- Dividend and bond yields fluctuate significantly over time. This means that a retiree's income will change from year to year. Volatile income makes budgeting nearly impossible.

- Natural income is highly unlikely to meet the spending pattern of most retirees once it's adjusted for inflation. Except for the very wealthy.

- Even if yield appears stable in percentage terms, the income received in monetary terms is in relation to the outstanding capital. This invariably fluctuates over the retirement period.

- Proponents of a natural yield retirement strategy have offered little empirical evidence to back their theory. They erroneously focus on the percentage yield of the FTSE 100 or FTSE All Share. Most retirees are more likely to have both bonds and shares in their portfolio.

The test

I set out to examine the natural yield approach to retirement income using empirical data. This time, I used the Barclays Equity Gilt Study (BEGS), which runs from 1900 to 2015. Unlike the DMS database which I used for my other research, BEGS decomposes equity and bond returns into capital growth and income yield.

- I created a portfolio consisting of 50% UK equities and 50% gilts, which is rebalanced annually.

- I examined the inflation-adjusted natural income on a £100,000 portfolio for retirement periods starting in 1900, 1905, 1910, 1915 .... to 2005 and 2010. I also included a retirement period starting in 2008, just to take my total number of scenarios to 20!

- Based on the dataset, I looked at a retirement period of 30 years. Retirees starting after 1985 haven't completed the full 30-year period yet, so I've presented their results for the period covered so far. For instance, a retirement period starting in 1990 (Class '90) has had 25 years so far and a retirement period starting in 2000 (Class '00) just 15 years!

- The real natural income is the inflation-adjusted natural income from the portfolio each year. I work on the basis that no withdrawal is taken from the capital and the retiree relies entirely on the natural dividends and coupon on their portfolio.

The result

Fig. 17 opposite shows the real income yield from the portfolio over the subsequent 30-year period (or less for retirement dates starting after 1985).

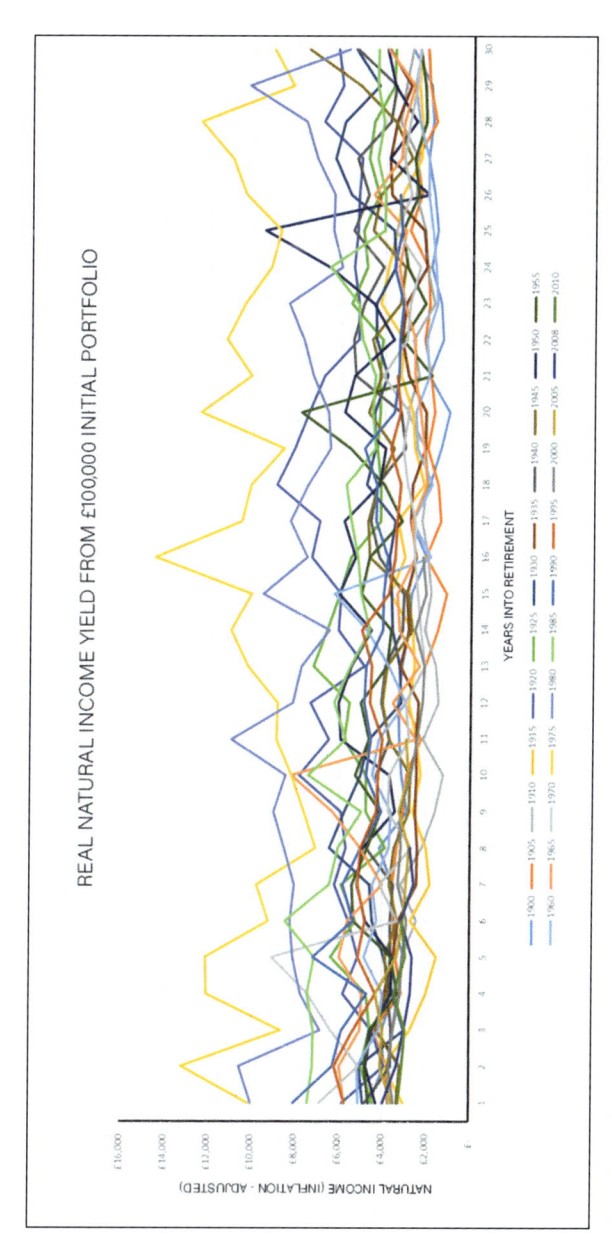

Fig. 17: Real (inflation-adjusted) natural income from £100,000 portfolio over subsequent 30 years from various start dates

This chart shows that a retiree relying only on natural income experiences significant income fluctuations from year to year.

For example, our Class of 1900 started their retirement with a natural income of £4,550. By the second year, their inflation-adjusted income fell to £3,897 and by the fifth year, it was £3,005. But their troubles had only just begun; by year 20, their real income had fallen to £1,024!

I don't know anyone who would find this level of income fluctuation acceptable.

In Fig. 18, I show the first year's natural income, the lowest, the mean and the highest real income over the entire retirement period. I also show the income volatility in percentage terms. This is the standard deviation from the mean income over each retirement period.

So, a retiree living off natural yield may or may not start off with a decent income. But they should expect their income to go up and down each year like a yo-yo. And once you add in the effect of inflation, this yo-yo effect (income volatility) is simply unacceptable for most people.

Chasing yield

Of course, an advocate of natural yield will argue that a natural yield portfolio will specifically overweight high-yield assets such as equities, commercial property, real estate

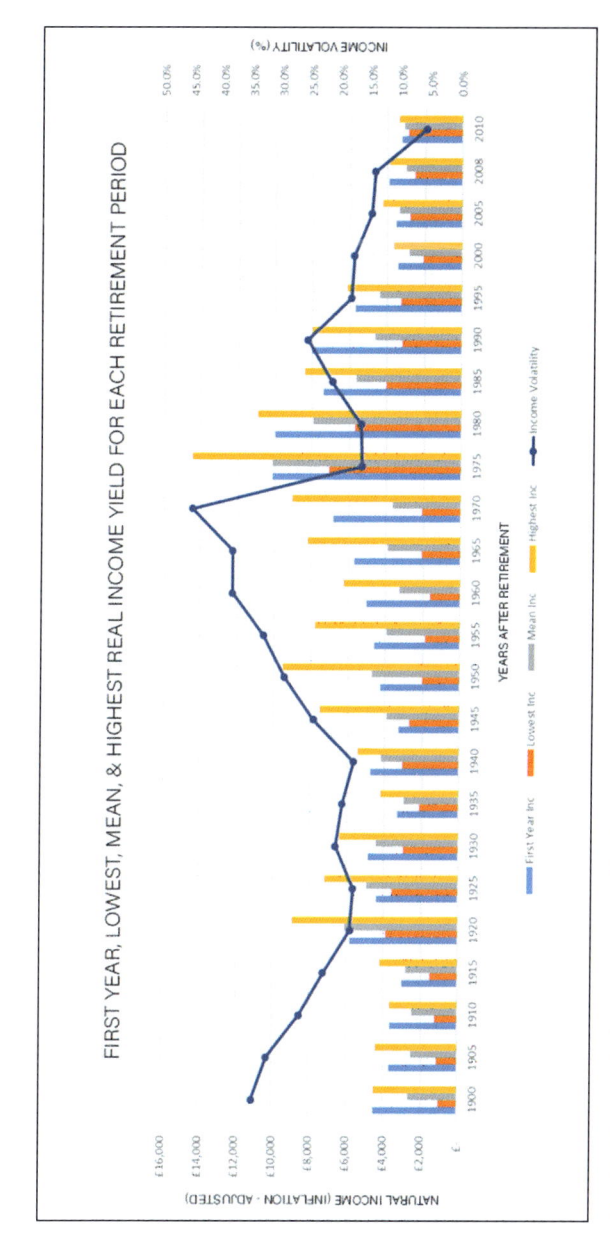

Fig. 18: First year's, lowest, mean and highest real natural income over the entire 30-year period for various start dates

Cumulative total returns during the global financial crisis, 12 October 2007 to 9 March 2009.

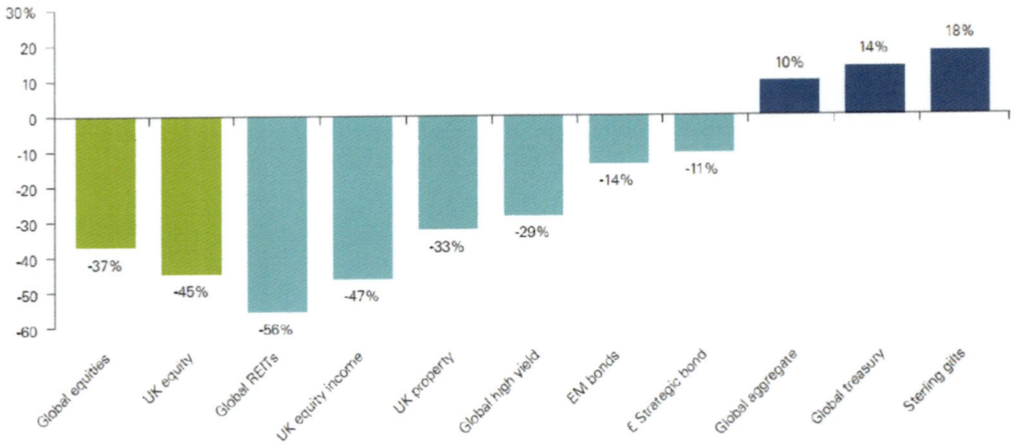

Global equities	-37%
UK equity	-45%
Global REITs	-56%
UK equity income	-47%
UK property	-33%
Global high yield	-29%
EM bonds	-14%
£ Strategic bond	-11%
Global aggregate	10%
Global treasury	14%
Sterling gilts	18%

Notes: Global equities are defined as the MSCI ACWI Index. UK equities are defined as the FTSE All-Share Index. UK equity income is defined as the FTSE 350 High Yield Index, commodities are defined as the S&P GSCI Index, global high yield is defined as the Barclays Global High Yield Index, EM bonds are defined as the Barclays Hard Currency Index, global REITs are represented by the Global Property Research World 250 REIT Index, UK property is represented by the CBRE UK Commercial Property Index, £ strategic bond is defined as the median return from the Morningstar Database from October 2007 to 26 February 2009, global corporate bonds are defined as the Barclays Global Corporate Index (hedged to GBP), global aggregate is defined as the Barclays Global Aggregate Index (hedged to GBP), global treasury bonds are defined as the Barclays Global Treasury Index (hedged to GBP), and gilts are defined as the Barclays Gilt Index. All returns are in sterling terms with income reinvested.

Sources: Vanguard calculations based on data from Barclays, Macrobond, and Morningstar Inc.

Fig. 19: Cumulative total returns during the global financial crisis (12 Oct., 2007 to Mar., 2009) investment trusts (REITs) and high-yield bonds. A paper by Vanguard[11] exposes the flaws in this thinking. I want to pick out these key drawbacks:

a) High-yield asset classes such as commercial property/REITs, equities and high-yield bonds tend to have large drawdowns, particularly during stressful market conditions. Fig. 19 is taken from the Vanguard paper referred to earlier and it shows the total returns of major asset classes, including high-yield ones during the financial crisis of 2008. As you can see, income-yielding asset classes experienced larger losses.

b) Overweighting high-yield asset classes invariably increases concentration risk and reduces diversification in the portfolio.

c) There's some empirical evidence to suggest that high dividend stocks tend to outperform over the very long term. This is essentially known as 'value premium.' But this is more likely to be down to a low price-to-dividend ratio (or frankly low price-to-anything ratio). Fortunately, there are better ways to capture value premium than price-to-dividends.Using price-to-earning or price-to-book is a far more effective way to capture the value premium.

d) The strategy relies heavily on the ability of a manager to select high-yield stocks and bonds. Good luck with that one.

---

11 Schlanger T., Jaconetti C., Westaway P., Daga A., (2016): Total-return investing: An enduring solution for low yields. Vanguard Research

I stand by my assertion that a natural yield approach is a bonkers retirement income strategy for virtually all but very wealthy retirees, who have other sources of steady income to rely on.

Cash is trash

Another common approach used by financial planners to manage sequence risk in retirement portfolios is to hold a cash reserve. The strategy typically involves holding between one to three years' worth of income in cash. This helps them to avoid having to sell down portfolio holdings to pay income during protracted market declines.

The question is, does a cash reserve enhance portfolio longevity better than a fully invested portfolio that sells down holdings to pay income? And with varying practices among planners, what is the optimal amount of cash holding in drawdown? I've seen one, two, three and even five years' worth of income held in cash reserves!

Holding lots of cash in a portfolio can be a drag on performance in the long run. For instance, based on 5%pa withdrawal rate, holding two years' of income equates to 10% of the portfolio (ignoring inflation and cash held to cover platform and advice fees), which could have been invested.

US-based financial planner Harold Evensky and his partner Deena Katz are perhaps the most prominent architects of the CFR strategy (Evensky-Katz Cash Flow Reserve Strategy). They've used it with clients and written about it for many years.

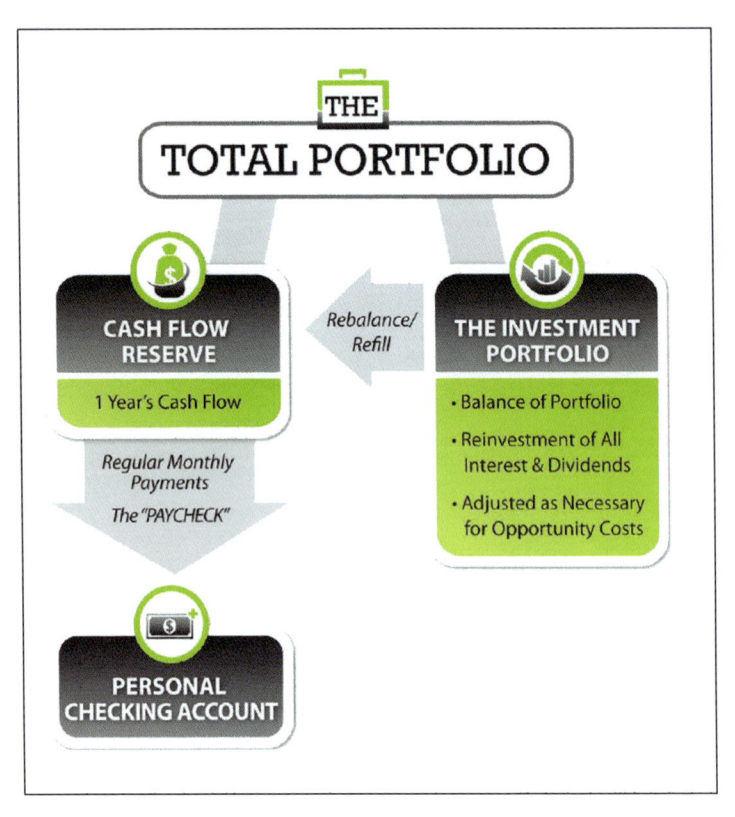

Fig. 20: Evensky- Katz Cash Flow Reserve Strategy

But does CFR strategy really work?

In a 2013 paper titled *The Benefits of a Cash Reserve Strategy in Retirement Distribution Planning*[12], Evensky et al used Monte Carlo simulations to compare a one-year CFR strategy with a fully invested 60/40 portfolio with no cash

---

12 Pfeiffer, Shaun, John Salter, and Harold Evensky. 2013. "The Benefits of a Cash Reserve Strategy in Retirement Distribution Planning." Journal of Financial Planning 26 (9): 49–55.

reserve. In the CFR, income is paid from the cash reserve and replenished if it dips below two months of income. The 60/40 portfolio is rebalanced annually, and the monthly income taken directly from the portfolio.

Based on a 4% withdrawal rate, they found that '*the fully invested portfolio is slightly superior to the cash reserve approach, assuming that there are no transaction costs and taxes.*' But when you take into account the transaction costs of selling down the portfolio monthly to pay income, the cash reserve approach produces a better outcome – around a 5% improvement in the success rate.

So, the cash reserve method doesn't help reduce the effects of sequence risk if there's no cost and tax drag for selling down the portfolio. Also, holding cash on most platforms results in negative return once you consider the platform fees. So, this diminishes the effectiveness of a cash reserve even further.

This finding is consistent with similar but more extensive research by Walter Woerheide and David Nanigian[13]. This used 83 years of historical data to test the success rate of one, two, three and four years' cash reserve vs. fully invested portfolios across several asset allocations and withdrawal rates.

---

13 Woerheide, Walter, and David Nanigian. 2012. "Sustainable Withdrawal Rates: The Historical Evidence on Buffer Zone Strategies." Journal of Financial Planning 25 (5): 46–52. Available at SSRN: https://ssrn.com/abstract=1969021 or http://dx.doi.org/10.2139/ssrn.1969021

In the CFR portfolios, they assumed that withdrawals were taken from the portfolios when return was positive and from the cash reserve when the portfolios were down. The overwhelming conclusion is that the fully invested portfolios produced better outcomes than corresponding cash reserve portfolios in about 80% of scenarios.

These studies appear to tell us that cash flow reserves don't necessarily help to mitigate sequencing risk. Using cash produces sub-optimal outcomes when compared to a fully invested portfolio. The reason is clear – markets tend to be up more than down, so trying to completely avoid volatility or being overly conservative doesn't compensate for the drag on returns. In any case, with a consistent rebalancing strategy, more of the withdrawals are taken from the asset class that's performed the best, assuming the withdrawal is pro-rated based on the portfolio allocation.

Sequence risk vs. stupidity risk

A cash reserve may not help with mitigating sequence risk but it could be very effective in reducing stupidity risk. It's hard to argue against the positive impact it has on managing the cognitive and behavioural biases that damage returns if retirees panic during market stress.

The knowledge that they always have six to 12 months' income in cash, which is not subject to the whims of the market, is an effective 'framing' and 'mental accounting' technique to help people sleep better at night during market declines. To quote Wall Street Journal columnist Jason Zweig, when markets fall, *'an investor who has courage but lacks cash is as powerless as one who has cash but no courage.'*

Yet it's important not to be overly conservative, as a lower allocation to equities invariably reduces a portfolio's longevity. Keeping more than one year of income in cash does more harm than good, and the trade-off in lost return is too high.

More importantly, this trade-off can be offset by taking the cash reserve from bond allocations, rather than the equity allocations. Suppose a 60/40 (equity/bond) portfolio is recommended for a client. If they keep 5% of the total portfolio in cash and invest £95,000 in a 60/40 portfolio, the overall allocation to equities is 57%. Instead, consider a 60/35/5%

allocation to equities/bond/cash. Woerheide and Nanigian's research indicates that if the cash reserve is taken from the bond allocation, no real harm is done (although no significant advantages are achieved). In other words, the cost of obtaining the behavioural benefits of a cash flow reserve is negligible.

It's important to think carefully about how frequently the cash reserve is replenished. Starting out with one year's income and replenishing the reserve every six months means you'll always have at least six months' worth of income in a cash reserve.

CHAPTER 4

Safe withdrawal rate: how safe?

The key framework for managing sequence risk from a drawdown portfolio originated from Bill Bengen. Bill was an engineer who later became a financial adviser. His seminal paper in 1994 transformed the conversation around retirement income planning. The paper has been peer-reviewed and referenced by both academics and practitioners.

Sadly, the SWR framework has been misinterpreted and misapplied far too often. If I didn't know better, I'd say Bill would be cringing if he read some of the nonsense that's been written.

Bengen's approach was to examine how to sustain spending. He didn't simply look at average rates of return, he examined actual historical sequences of market returns. He established a safe withdrawal rate (SWR) – a percentage of the initial balance, with the ongoing withdrawal amount adjusted for inflation. It was capable of surviving any 30-year sequence in history. It's crucial to understand that the percentage of withdrawal only relates to the capital in the first year of retirement. So, for instance, a withdrawal rate of 4% from a £100,000 portfolio gives an income of £4,000 in the first year. This £4,000 a year then increases or decreases in line with inflation each year, regardless of the value of the outstanding portfolio.

SWR is based on the most severe economic and market conditions in 100 years of market history. And it's designed to survive these extreme conditions.

Adapting Bengen's approach to the UK, the SWR is 3.1%. This is based on someone who started their 30-year retirement in 1900. But other 30-year periods starting in 1901, 1902, 1903, 1936 and 1947 were equally bad.

Important facts about Bengen's safe withdrawal rate framework:

1. The SWR is the worst-case historical scenario

One way to visualise this is to apply the SWR of 3.1% to a portfolio of £100,000 over every 30-year period starting in 1900-1929, 1901-1930 to 1986-2016. Fig. 22 shows the year-end balance of 87 individual 30-year scenarios. The worst-case scenario is highlighted in red.

In 80% of the 30-year historical scenarios (68 out of 87 rolling 30-year periods), if a retiree used the SWR framework, they would have ended up with more capital, in nominal terms, than they started with after 30 years of withdrawal. This highlights the cautious nature of the SWR framework. It means that the framework is designed to survive some of the most severe market conditions. It's as safe as you can get

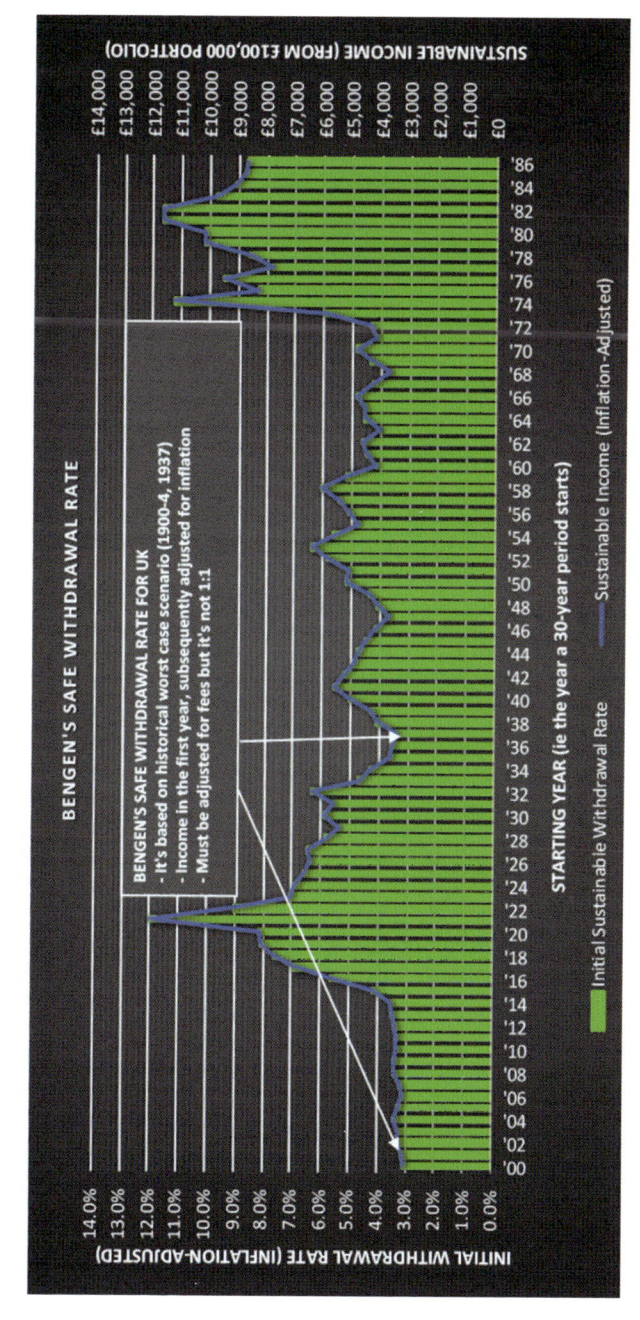

Fig. 21: Bengen's safe withdrawal rate using UK Equities and Bonds

85

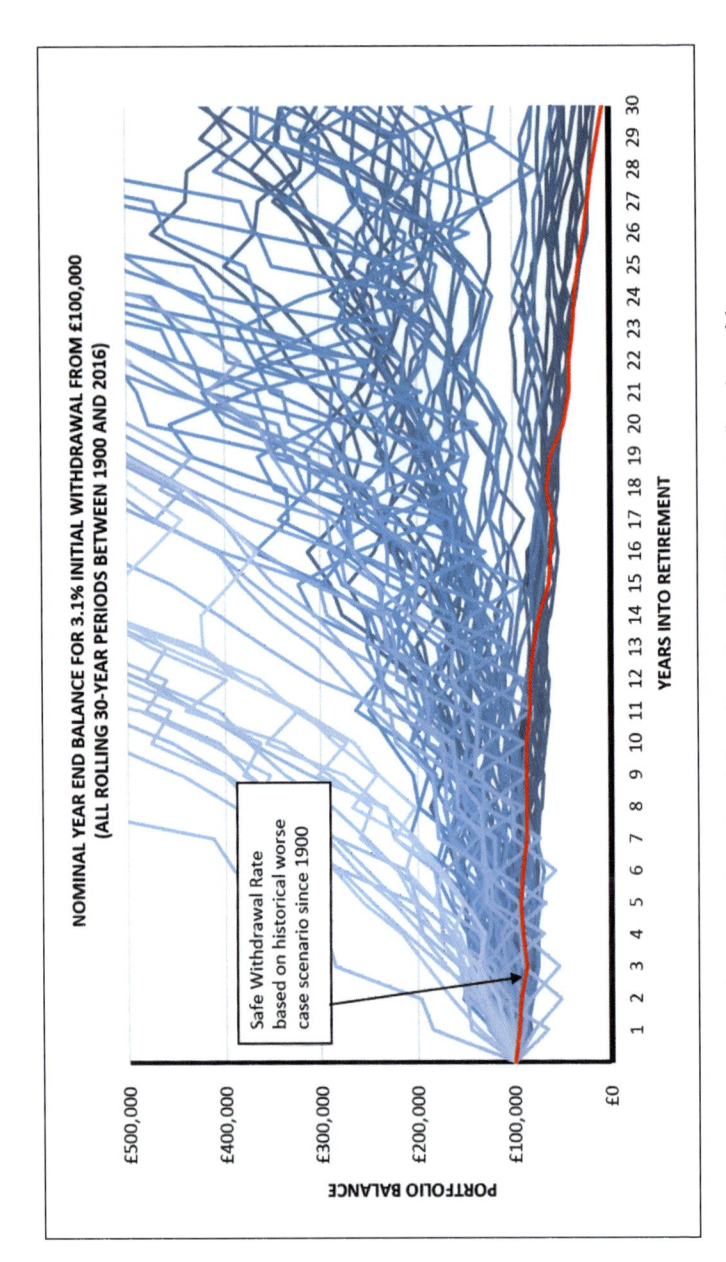

Fig. 22: Nominal year-end balance under safe withdrawal rate for a 50/50 UK equity/bond portfolio

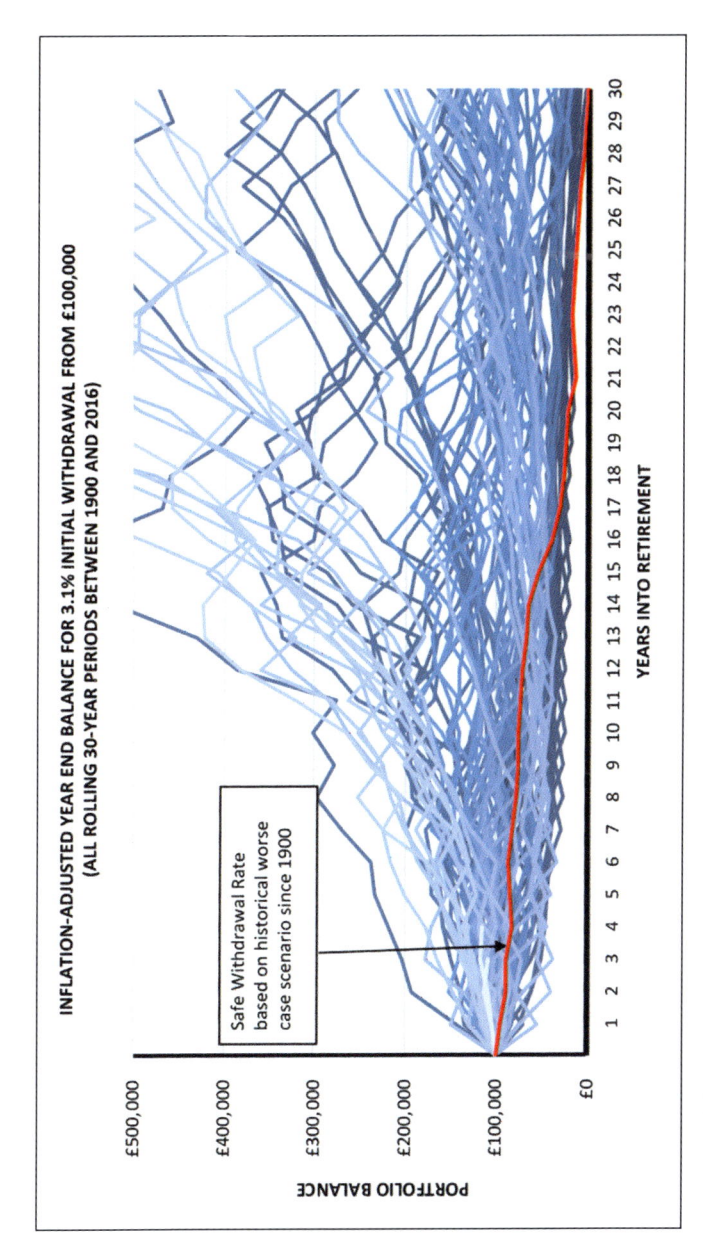

Fig. 23: Real (inflation-adjusted) year-end balance under safe withdrawal rate for a 50/50 UK equity/bond portfolio

with the capital markets. The other alternative is for clients to spend less or die sooner!

2. Inflation-adjusted income

One crucial (but often forgotten) point about Bengen's framework is that the SWR is defined only as a percentage of the capital in the first year. Subsequent monetary withdrawals are adjusted for inflation, regardless of the outstanding balance in future years. So, the actual withdrawal rate in percentage terms will change from year to year as the outstanding balance and annual income in monetary terms adjusts. But the real inflation-adjusted income in monetary terms remains the same as the income in the first year!

Bengen's approach is the complete opposite of what many people think it is – ie, taking a percentage of their outstanding portfolio each year. Doing this would make budgeting nearly impossible, thanks to significant fluctuations in actual income from year to year. For instance, if you took 4% of a £100,000 portfolio in the first year, you'd have an income of £4,000. If the portfolio value has dropped to £90,000 in the second year, 4% of the portfolio gives an income of £3,600. If the portfolio recovers in the third year and it's now worth £110,000, taking 4% gives you an income of £4,400. And of course, this may or may not keep up with inflation.

Bengen's approach avoids these scenarios where income goes up and down like a yo-yo. That's why he defined SWR only in terms of the first year's income and capital. Bengen's baseline SWR gives retirees the same inflation-adjusted income throughout the entire period. (We'll discuss whether this is appropriate or not later.)

Fig. 24 and Fig. 25 show the nominal and inflation-adjusted annual income for Bengen's baseline approach, depending on the retirement date.

Fig. 25 opposite, which shows the inflation-adjusted income for all the historical scenarios, isn't a mistake. It's really a single line! This is because Bengen's aim is to maintain the initial income throughout retirement.

3. The oft-cited '4% rule' was created with a US investor in mind, and should not be applied blindly to the UK (or any other country for that matter)

As Fig. 26 by Professor Wade Pfau shows, the SWR for the UK is lower than the US. This is because the American market is much deeper than the UK. Historically, long-term returns tend to be higher for equities and bonds. US equities have an average of 1% real return above the UK. The US bond market has an average of 0.5% real return above the UK.

4. The exact rate will vary depending on the asset allocation

Bengen's original research is based on a 50/50 equity-bond portfolio. He strongly recommended that equity allocation

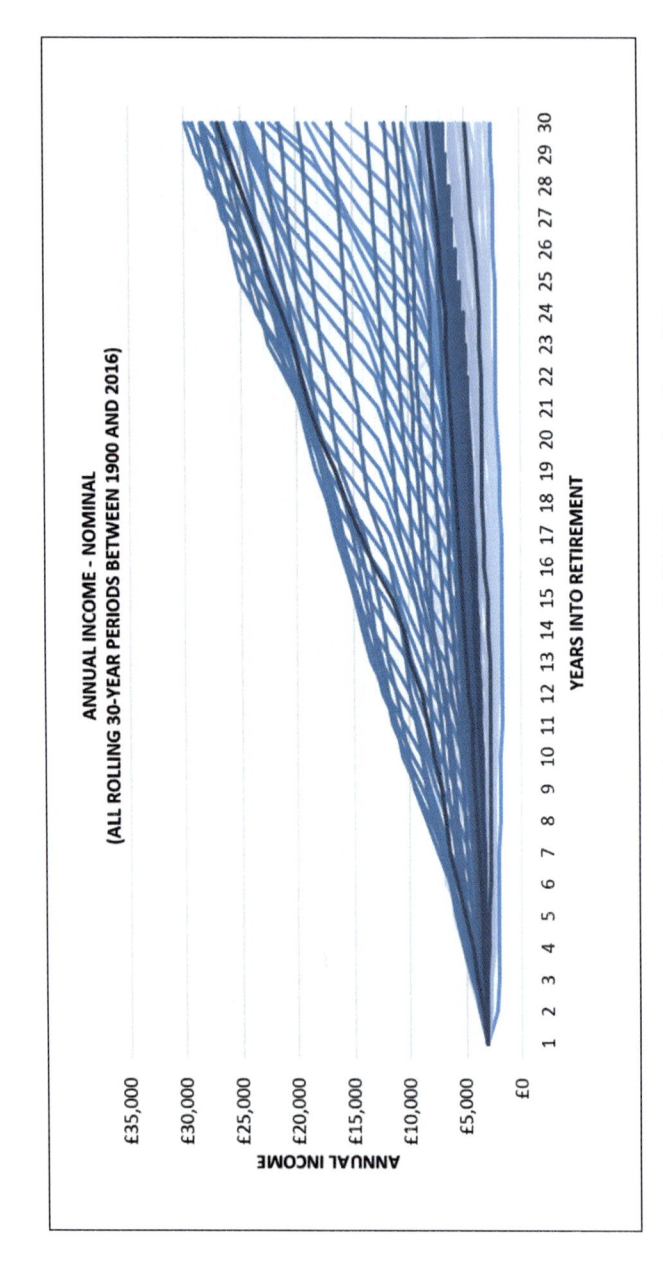

Fig. 24: Nominal annual income under safe withdrawal rate for a 50/50 UK equity/bond portfolio

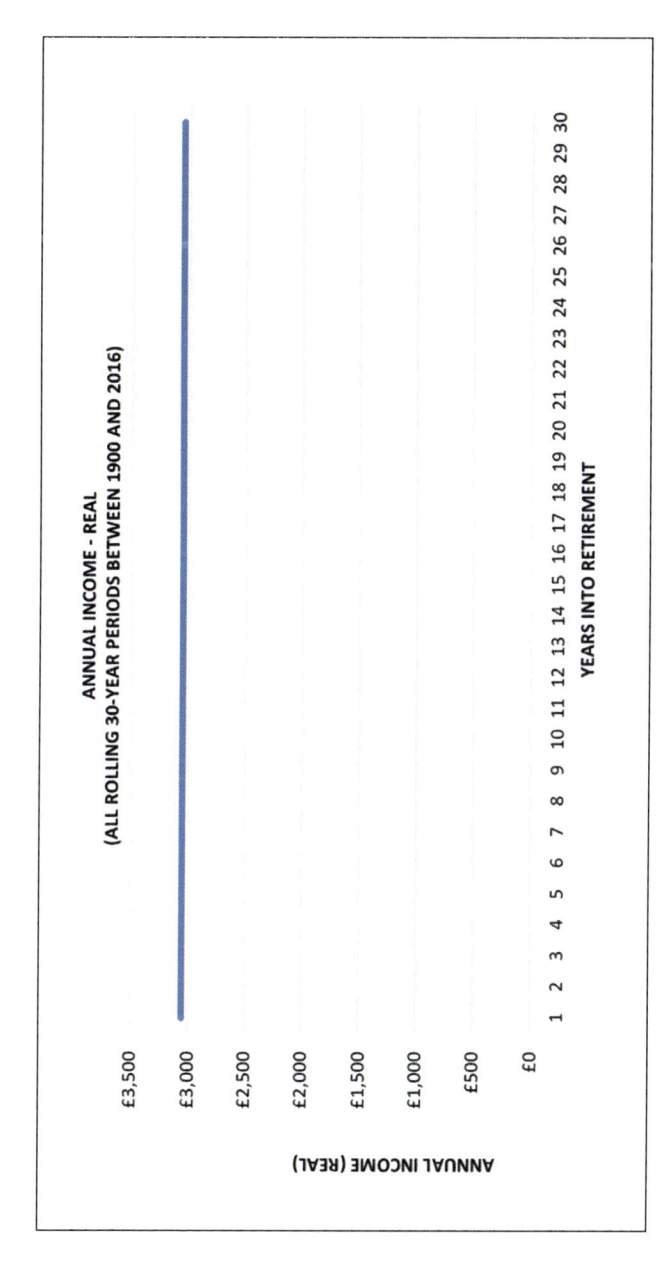

Fig. 25: Real annual income under safe withdrawal rate for a 50/50 UK equity/bond portfolio

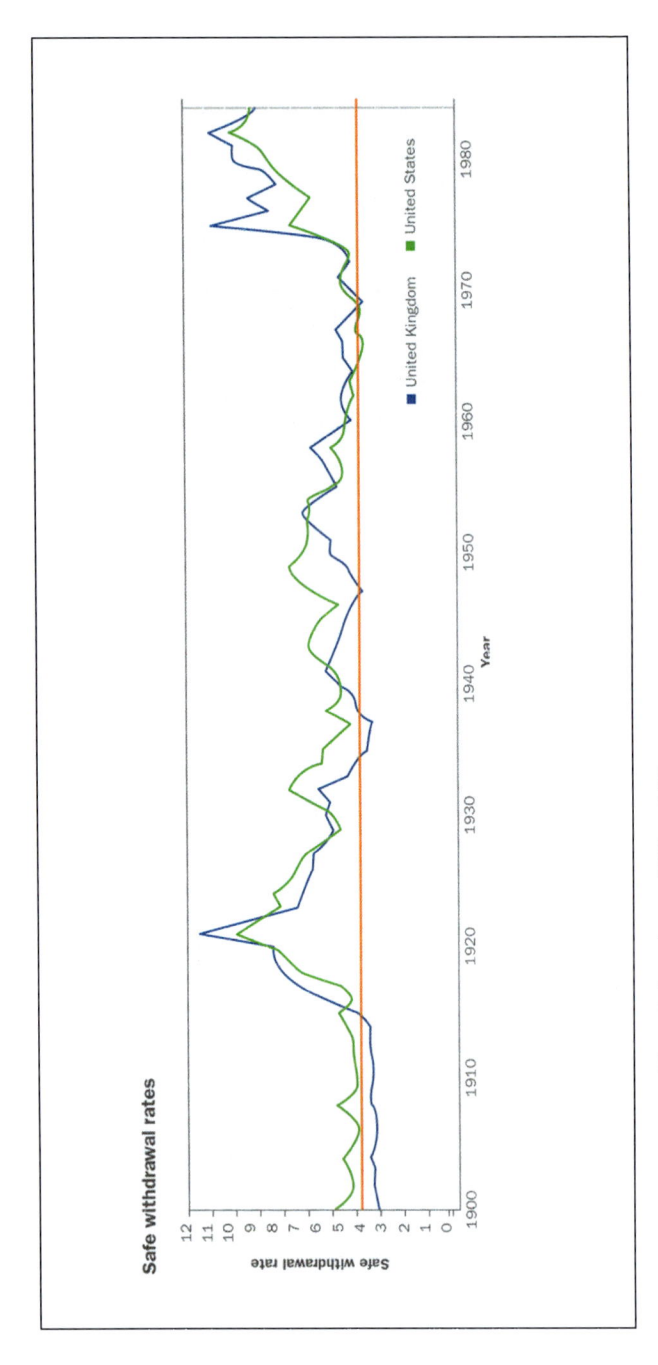

Fig. 26: Maximum sustainable withdrawal rate (UK vs. US)

in a retirement portfolio should be no less than 50% and no more than 75%.

Asset allocation plays a crucial role in determining the SWR for each retiree. There's a consensus that generally, the greater the allocation to equities, the higher the SWR. However, the client's risk profile should play a vital role in deciding the asset allocation.

We'll return to this subject later.

5. The SWR should be adapted to take account of investment and product fees

This adjustment is not a 1:1. So, a fee of 1% will not necessarily result in a 1% reduction in SWR.

Fig. 27 below shows that a 1% fee reduces the SWR for a 50/50 UK portfolio from 3.10% to 2.6%. This is a reduction of 0.5%.

My findings are similar to research[14] by Pye (2001) and Kitces, (2010) who found a reduction of 0.45% in the SWR for every 1% fee.

---

14 Pye, Gordon B. "Adjusting Withdrawal Rates for Taxes and Expenses". Journal of Financial Planning, April 2001.
Kitces, Michael E. "Investment Costs, Taxes, and the Safe Withdrawal Rate". The Kitces Report, February 2010

This may appear odd at first, but when you think about it, it makes sense. The SWR is based on the initial portfolio balance, while the percentage-of-assets fee is based on the portfolio balance each subsequent year.

The portfolio balance is depleted over time, as income withdrawal is adjusted for inflation – at least under poor market conditions. This means that the actual fee deducted is a percentage of a falling portfolio size. More importantly, the percentage-of-assets-based fee naturally adjusts downwards as a portfolio is spent.

6. Bengen's SWR works on the basis that withdrawal will be adjusted for inflation (up or down) every year regardless of what happens to the portfolio balance

Retirees who don't intend to adjust their withdrawal for inflation are able to enjoy a higher withdrawal rate, at least in the early part of their retirement. (More on this in the next chapter.)

The SWR gives us a framework to think about risk when drawing retirement income. It's not the set-and-forget approach that some people think it is. The key is to understand the framework and the factors that play a role rather than obsessing about exact withdrawal rates.

The main weakness of Bengen's SWR is the assumption that people will maintain the same level of real spending throughout their retirement. It assumes that retirees will

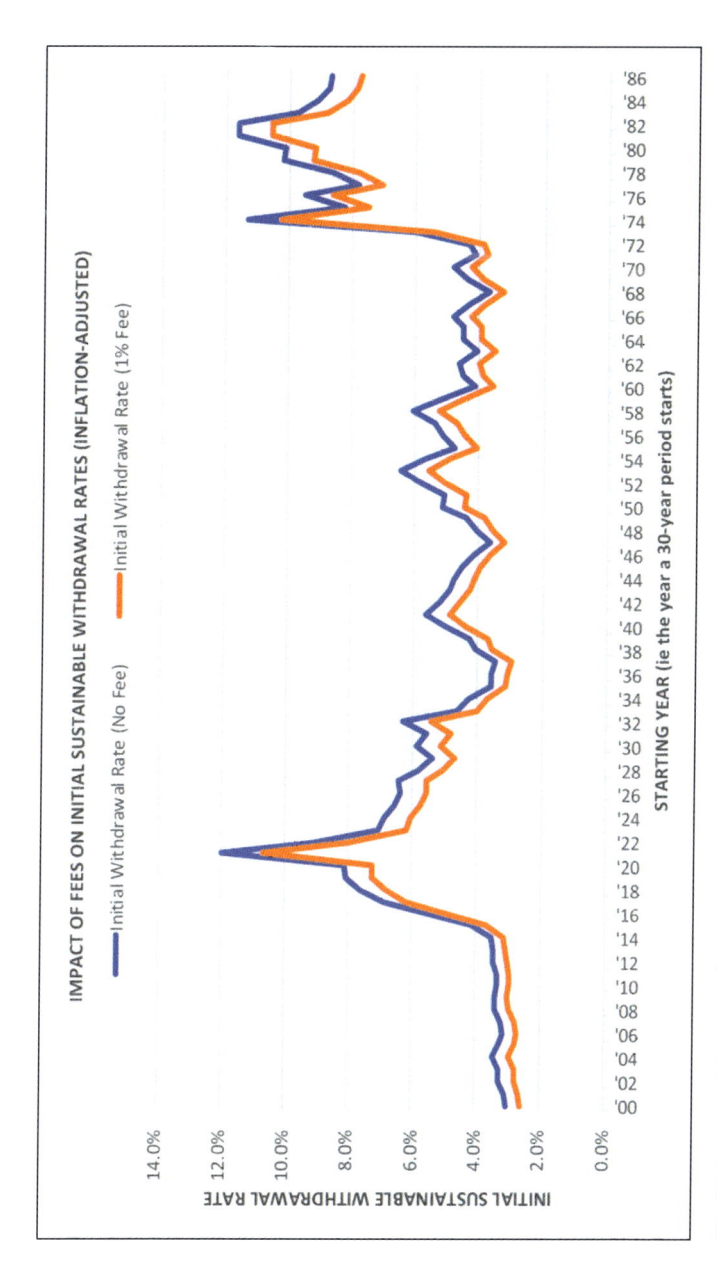

Fig. 27: Impact of fees on inflation-adjusted sustainable withdrawal rate

play a game of chicken with their portfolio by increasing their withdrawal with inflation every single year, while their portfolio plummets to zero. But real spending tends to fall gradually in retirement.

Also, the constant inflation-adjusted withdrawal is inefficient because it's based on the very worst-case scenario in market history. In nearly 80% of historical scenarios, after a 30-year period, the baseline SWR would have resulted in a retiree ending up with more money than they started with. This means the SWR forces retirees to leave money on the table under favourable market conditions, when they could have spent more during their lifetimes.

Some people have adapted the SWR to help capture more of the upside, by taking a higher withdrawal rate and having safeguards to prevent unsustainable withdrawals. These are known as rule-based withdrawal strategies. These strategies allow retirees to start with a higher level of withdrawal and adjust their spending gradually downwards if they face poor returns in the early part of their retirement. (As we know, returns in the first decade of retirement have a significant impact on the overall outcome of a 30-year retirement.)

I cover these strategies in more detail in Chapter 6.

Could future market conditions ruin safe withdrawal rate?

The answer is yes, there's a possibility this could happen, but things would have to be really bad. It's worth exploring the market conditions that created the SWR framework in the first place.

The market conditions that created SWR

In the UK, the SWR is based on hypothetical individuals starting their withdrawal in 1901 or 1937. The historical model highlights four particular periods in the UK's 115-year market history where the SWR would have been no more than 3.1% (before fees) – those starting a 30-year retirement between 1900-1908 and 1936-1939.

I'd like to explore market conditions for the individual starting out in 1937. We'll call her 'Mrs 1937'.

Mrs 1937 would have started her retirement during the worst possible period in living memory: bang in the middle of two world wars and a period of extreme political instability.

Britain's economy was already struggling in the 1920s, having borrowed so much to pay for the First World War.

Then the Great Depression hit the US in 1929 and reached the UK shortly after. The UK stock market plummeted, and by

1931, unemployment was at a record level. It was 20% nationally, but parts of the country witnessed up to 60% unemployment. Britain's export revenue halved and the government of the day was forced to come off the Gold Standard in 1931. During this period, Britain's Debt to National Income Ratio was more than 200%!

In 1932, in the grip of the Great Depression, Britain (and France) defaulted on First World War debt to the United States – the so-called inter-allied debt. Britain had linked the end of paying off these debts to the premature end of German reparation payments earlier in the year. Academics have therefore termed this an 'excusable default' where Germany was the real defaulter. The default was done without consent[15].

Records at the Office of the Historian at the US Department of State note, *'After the November 1932 election of Franklin D. Roosevelt, France and the United Kingdom resurrected the link between reparations and war debts, tying their Lausanne Conference pledge to cancel their claims against Germany to the cancellation of their debts to the United States. The United States would not accept the proposal. By mid-1933, all European debtor nations except Finland had defaulted on their loans from the United States'*[16].

---

[15] Jim Leaviss (2010) What happened the last time the UK defaulted? https://www.bondvigilantes.com/blog/2010/02/02/what-happened-the-last-time-the-uk-defaulted/

[16] The Dawes Plan, the Young Plan, German Reparations, and Inter-allied War Debts https://history.state.gov/milestones/1921-1936/dawes

COULD FUTURE MARKET CONDITIONS RUIN SAFE WITHDRAWAL RATE?

The UK stock market started to recover around the mid-1930s, only for another recession to hit, just as Mrs 1937 was about to start her retirement. This was followed by the threat of another World War. In 1938, a year into Mrs 1937's retirement, the Prime Minister Neville Chamberlain met Adolf Hitler in Munich. He came back with the news that he'd averted a war with Germany. The next year, Germany invaded Poland, and the UK declared war on Germany. And so World War Two broke out.

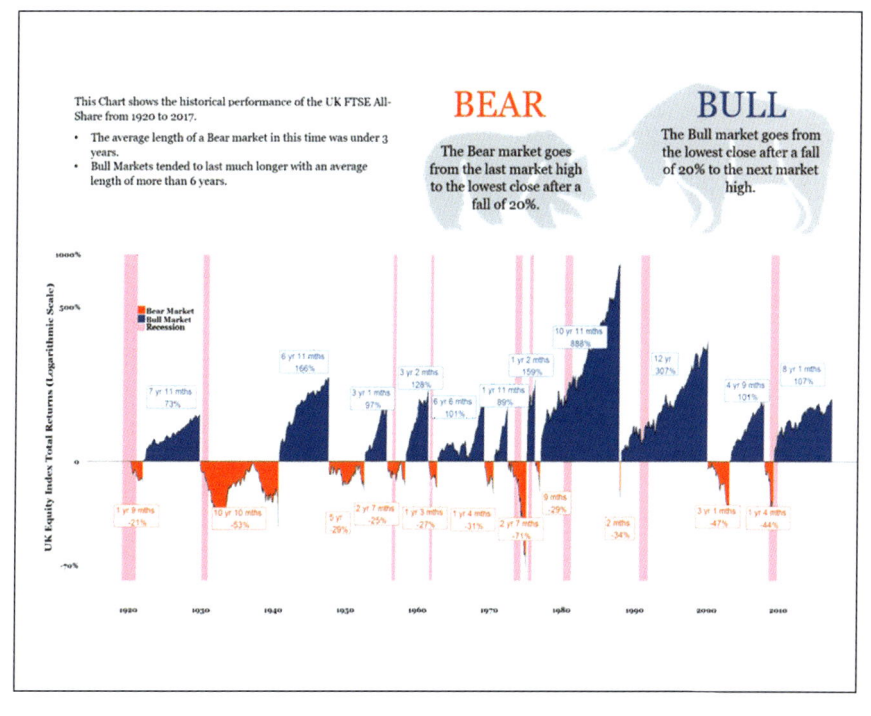

Fig. 28: History of UK equity bull and bear markets since 1920

So, Mrs 1937 would have seen her portfolio fall massively in the first few years of her retirement. This period, starting in 1937, was the only period I found over the last 115 years where the UK stock market fell for four consecutive years. There was also a very high rate of inflation in the first four years of her retirement.

From the peak of the market in 1936 through to 1940, the FTSE 30 fell by over 60%! But Mrs 1937 wouldn't have run out of money over a 30-year period if she'd adopted the SWR framework.

These are the kind of severe market conditions that created the SWR framework and show just how bad things would have to get for it to fail.

How has SWR held up since the tech bubble and the 2008 financial crisis?

It's also worth considering how the SWR has held up in other severe market conditions.

It's actually held up pretty well, particularly during the tech bubble and the 2008 financial crisis.

Retirees who started out in 2000 and 2008 haven't completed a full 30-year retirement period yet. But, it's possible to compare the glide path of their portfolio balances at various points with one from someone who retired under the 1900 or 1937 scenarios.

You can see in Fig. 29 that if you started retirement in the middle of the 2000 tech bubble, or the 2008 financial crisis, your portfolio has fared much better than the 1900 and 1937 scenarios that created the SWR.

In fact, anyone who started their retirement in 2000 or 2008 adopting the SWR framework would have higher account balances six years and 15 years into their retirement than the retiree that created the SWR in the first place!

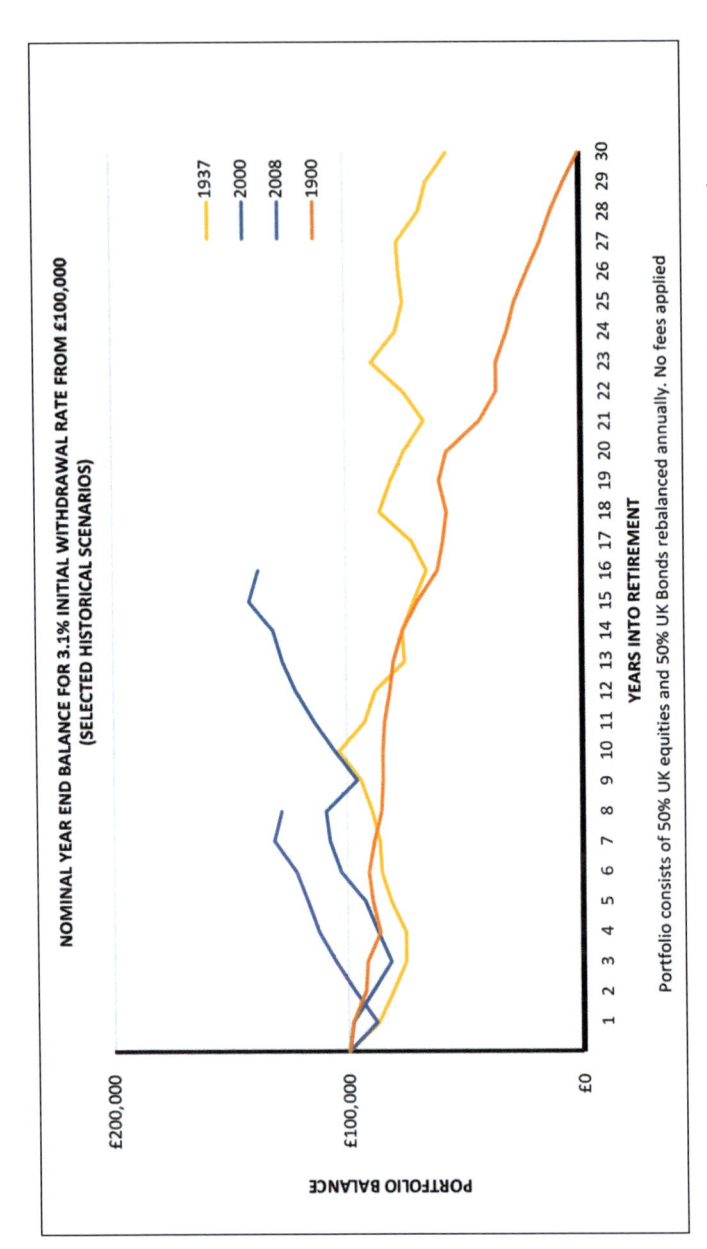

Fig. 29: Portfolio values through retirement using 3.1% Initial Sustainable Withdrawal Rate with various start dates

What's the impact on alternative retirement income products?

It is also worth considering the potential impact of such severe market conditions on other alternative retirement income products, such as annuities and guaranteed drawdown.

A market condition so severe as to ruin the SWR framework is also likely to cause the failure of annuity providers! People often tell me this claim is an exaggeration to support the robustness of SWR. But less than a decade ago, the 2008/9 financial crisis forced the US government to set up the Troubled Asset Relief Programme (TARP) to stop AIG and several insurers/annuity providers in the US from going belly up. But someone who started their retirement during the same period and adopted the SWR framework is faring rather well so far.

I believe a severe economic situation that would ruin the SWR framework would probably cause the collapse of the Financial Services Compensation Scheme (FSCS). Severe economic conditions in the 1930s caused the UK Government to default on its inter-allied war debt to the US. So, it's not inconceivable that the UK government would be unable to back the FSCS or protect annuity holders in even worse market conditions.

The FSCS has no reserve. It relies on a levy on the financial sector to meet compensation requirements. During the

2008 financial crisis, the FSCS borrowed £20.4bn from HM Treasury to fund the cost of compensating consumers whose savings were put at risk by the failures[17]. If there was another severe market downturn, there's no reason to believe the FSCS in its current form would be any better equipped to meet compensation demands.

The SWR is the most robust withdrawal framework financial planning has come up with. Other than telling clients to spend less... or just die sooner!

Finally, it's important to realise that the SWR is only meant to be a framework. It's a crude but robust guide. A good financial planner will adapt this framework based on the requirements of the client, fees, asset allocation, etc. For example, they may start with a higher withdrawal rate but adjust dynamically depending on market conditions.

---

[17] Refinancing of loans for 2008/09 bank failures http://www.fscs.org.uk/industry/news/2012/march/refinancing-of-loans-for-2008-0-v6tamywr/

CHAPTER 5

Busting the myth of U-shaped retirement spending

If I had a pound for every time someone in financial services talks about spending in retirement as being U-shaped, I'd never have to work again!

You've probably seen this image of spending needs in retirement before. It's a commonly held view that most people spend more early in retirement when they're active and keen to enjoy their new-found freedom. Spending declines when they move into a less-active phase, only for it to pick up dramatically in later life due to care costs.

Sounds logical, right?

The trouble is, for the majority of people, this idea of U-shaped spending in retirement is just a big fat myth.

For some time, researchers have identified an important phenomenon known as the *saving puzzle*. Older people keep saving once they've retired and the amount increases with age!

Spending needs in retirement
Expenditure = ▬

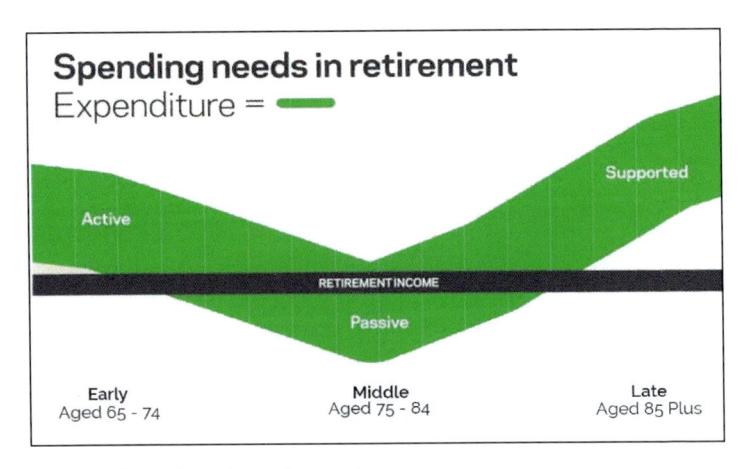

Supported
Active
RETIREMENT INCOME
Passive

| Early | Middle | Late |
| Aged 65 - 74 | Aged 75 - 84 | Aged 85 Plus |

Fig. 30: The U-shaped spending path in retirement

Dr Brancati and her colleagues at the International Longevity Center - UK analysed two large datasets, the Living Costs and Food Survey and the English Longitudinal Study of Ageing. They wanted to gain insight into the older population's income and expenditure patterns. Their findings are in a paper called *Understanding Retirement Journeys: Expectations vs reality*[18]. The researchers note the absence of the U-shaped spending in retirement.

'*Our findings suggest that typical consumption in retirement does not follow a U-shaped path – consumption does not dramatically rise at the start of retirement or pick up towards the end of life to meet long-term care-related expenditures. At this point, it should be noted that our data is restricted to households only and therefore excludes those actively living in care homes who may be paying for it from*

---

[18] ILC (2015) Understanding retirement journeys: expectations vs reality. International Longevity Centre

their remaining assets. Yet we can explore the extent to which care expenditures eat into household budgets across different ages. Analysis of the data suggests that even for the 80+ age group, only a minority (6.4% of households) are putting money towards meeting long-term care needs. This doesn't mean that U-shaped consumption in retirement is a misnomer but perhaps implies that it is atypical.'

It turns out, as people get older, they spend progressively less.

'A household headed by someone age 80+ spends, on average, 43% (or £131) less than a household headed by a 50-year-old. If we include the amount of money people pay for their mortgage as household expenditure, then the decline becomes even steeper with households headed by someone aged 80+ spending 56.4% less (or £173) than households headed by a 50-year-old. Indeed, we calculate that by age 80+, individuals are saving, on average, around £5,870 per year!'

Fig. 31 overleaf shows that, from age 65, spending typically declines progressively and is about 35% lower at age 80.

Even when researchers split people aged 50+ between top and bottom earners (ie people whose income is either above or below the median), the trend remains broadly consistent. People spend progressively less as they get older. However, high earners experience a much faster and steeper decline in spending after age 60 than bottom earners. Bottom earners have more stable spending patterns throughout their lifetime, and their total expenditure starts to decline only after age 70.

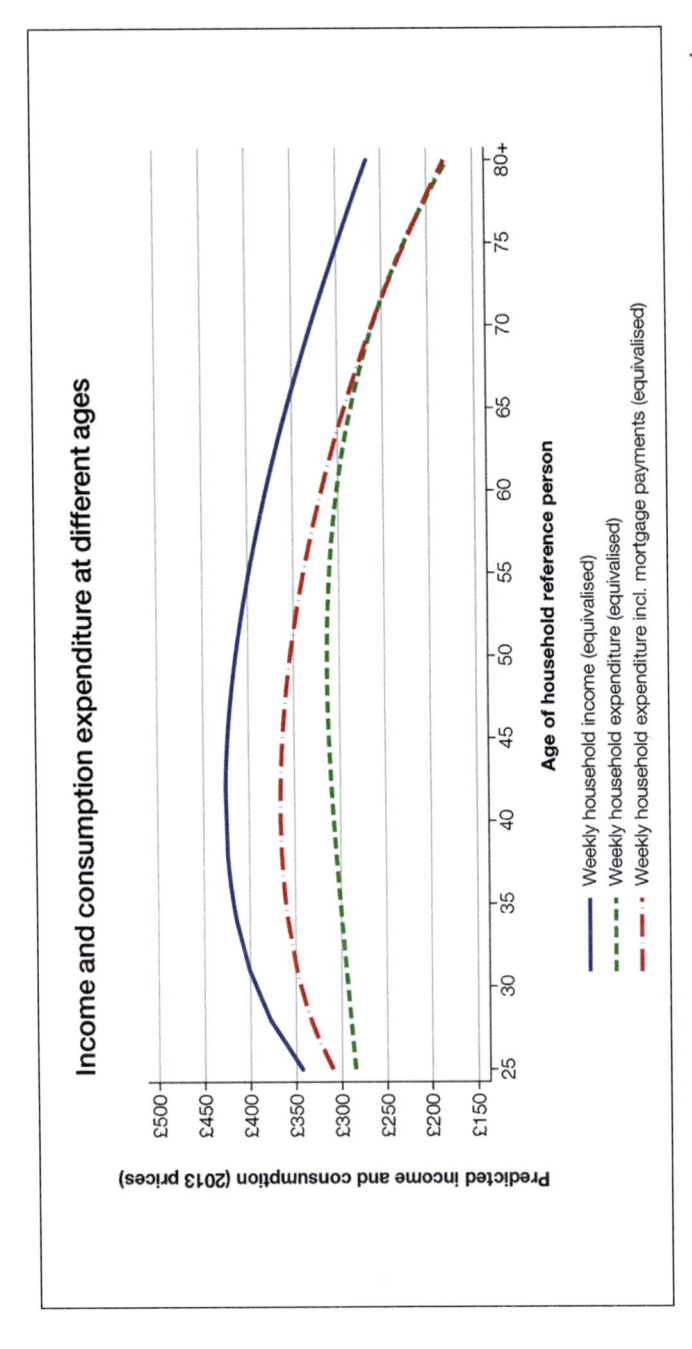

Fig. 31: Income and consumption expenditure at different ages. Source: ILC (2015) Understanding retirement journeys: expectations vs. reality.

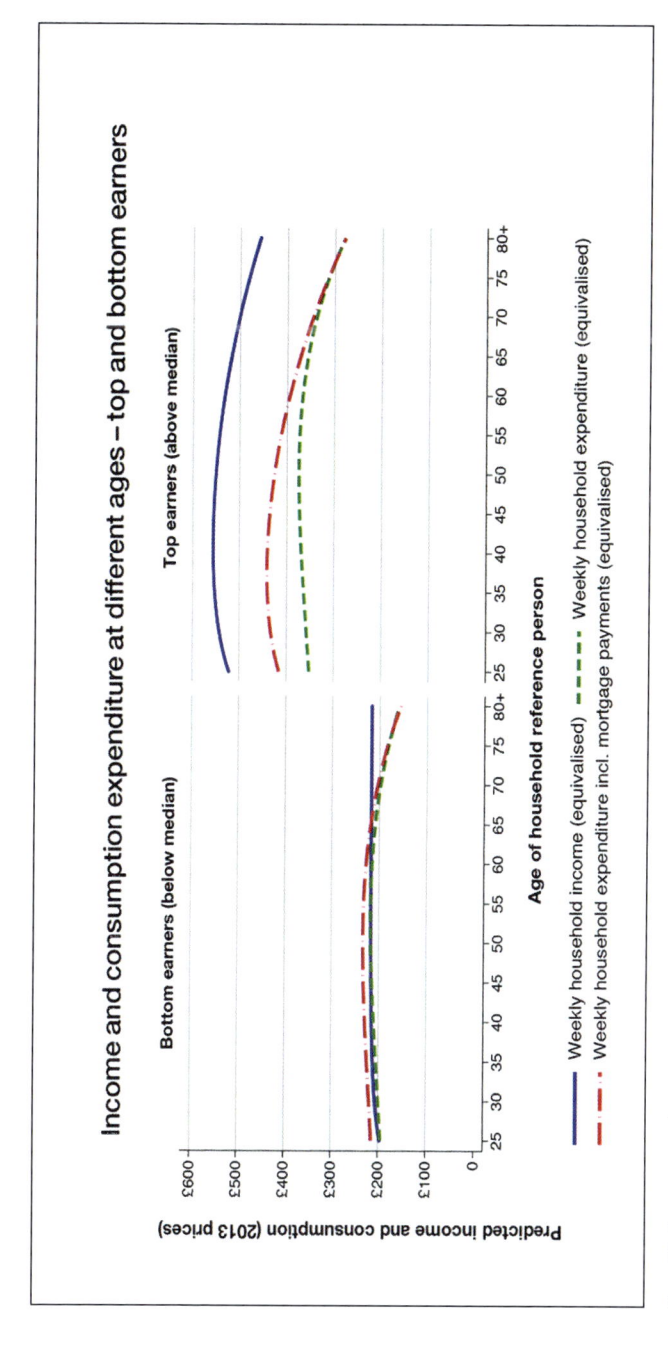

Fig. 32: Income and consumption expenditure at different ages – top and bottom earners. Source: ILC (2015) Understanding retirement journeys: expectations vs. reality.

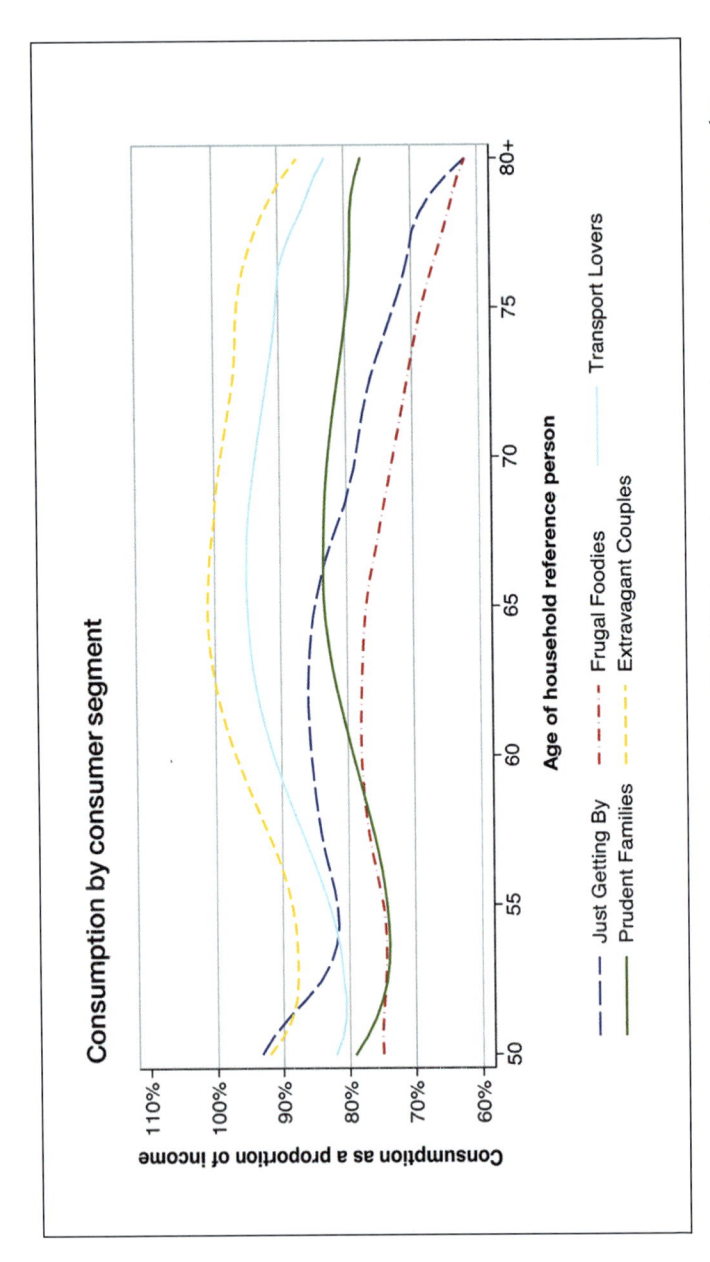

Fig. 33: Consumption by consumer segment. Source: ILC (2015) Understanding retirement journeys: expectations vs. reality

The authors concluded that older people spend consistently less than their younger counterparts regardless of their income. This trend is persistent, and it's not a periodic effect.

'Consumption in retirement starts relatively high and ends low. This pattern is common to both high and low-income groups, is robust to the inclusion of factors other than age and is not simply the result of the time period in which the data was collected.'

Amazingly, this trend is broadly consistent even when you look at people with different lifestyles. The authors note that even the 'Extravagant Couples' – those who spend nearly 40% of their total expenditure on recreational goods and services – spend more than their income in the first decade or so of retirement, as do those who are 'Just Getting By', The 'Prudent Families' and 'Frugal Foodies' consistently spend below their income over the duration of their retirement.

All of the groups save in later life. From age 75 onwards, even the 'Just Getting By' group, which is the lowest income group, starts to save. This is because they spend less on non-essential items towards the end of life.

These findings are consistent with findings[19] in the US, where researchers found that retirement spending tends to decrease by at least 1% a year in real terms throughout retirement!

Additional research by JP Morgan Chase (2015)[20] shows that, even for high-net worth (HNW) households (US), spending in retirement tends to decline as they get older. Care costs jump in later life but not enough to upend decline in other discretionary expenses.

Of course, many people will need care in later life, but this isn't typical. Consider the following data from Age UK (2016)[21.]

- Only 16% of people aged 85+ in the UK live in care homes.

- The median period from admission to the care home to death is 462 days. (15 months)

- Around 27% of people lived in care homes for more than three years.

- Approximately 30% of people use some form of local authority-funded social care in the last year of life.

---

19 Blanchett, David, Estimating the True Cost of Retirement. Morningstar, 2013. http://corporate.morningstar.com/ib/documents/MethodologyDocuments/ResearchPapers/Blanchett_True-Cost-of-Retirement.pdf

20 JP Morgan Chase (2015) Spending In Retirement https://am.jpmorgan.com/us/institutional/library/retirement-spending

21 Age UK (2016) Later Life in the United Kingdom December 2016

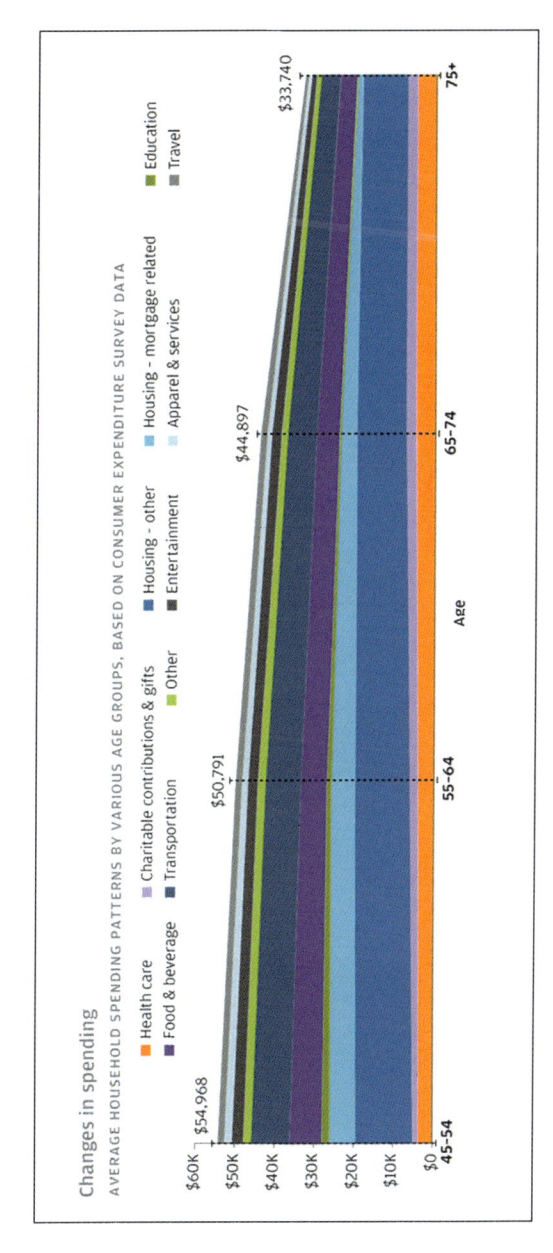

Fig. 34: Average spending pattern of various age groups (Chase Households with $1-$2million in assets)

It's important to factor possible care costs into a retirement income plan, but the chances that someone actually ends up having to pay for care are relatively low. In any case, it's entirely practical for people to rely on their property wealth to meet care costs in later life. And while it may not always be ideal, local authority-funded social care remains the last resort under current law.

So what?

The assumption that income withdrawal needs to keep up with inflation throughout the entire retirement period is not supported by empirical data on spending patterns in retirement. This has a major implication for how we calculate sustainable withdrawal from retirement portfolios.

An ideal sustainable withdrawal strategy should follow the typical spending pattern in retirement. This allows higher withdrawal at the early part of retirement and should progressively fall (at least in real terms) over their retirement period.

A major weakness of Bill Bengen's SWR is that it assumes expenditure remains constant in real terms throughout retirement. This is inconsistent with research findings on how consumption actually changes in retirement.

Thankfully, a range of flexible withdrawal strategies has been developed to reflect likely changes in retirement spending.

CHAPTER 6

SWR 2.0: the power of flexible withdrawal strategies

'Luck is not a strategy.'

– James Francis Cameron

Since Bengen's original research in 1994, numerous studies have expanded the SWR framework to incorporate additional factors. I call this SWR 2.0.

In this section, I want to explore a number of rule-based withdrawal strategies. They aim to identify simple adjustments to withdrawal that mean money lasts a lifetime, but without excessive income volatility. Crucially, these strategies mean withdrawal can match the typical consumption path in retirement more closely.

There are several withdrawal rules – too many to discuss and model. I'll focus on six different flexible withdrawal strategies. We can broadly classify them under two categories:

- inflation adjustment
- advance withdrawal rules

Inflation adjustment is a rule-based approach to how to adjust withdrawals for inflation each year. Advanced withdrawal strategies make further adjustments to the withdrawal over and above inflation adjustments.

Baseline	Bengen's constant inflation adjustment (CIA)
Inflation adjustment	Fixed withdrawal – no inflation adjustment
	Guyton inflation adjustment
	Cap and collar inflation adjustment
Advanced withdrawal rules	Guardrails strategy
	Ratcheting strategy
	Floor & ceiling strategy

Fig. 35: Rule-based sustainable withdrawal strategies

In practice, you can combine the advanced withdrawals with any of the inflation-adjustment rules. This gives a total of 16 strategies. Four inflation-adjustments (including Bengen's CIA) on their own and 12 more combinations of advanced and inflation-adjustment rules.

For simplicity, I only discuss seven strategies in this book:

SWR 2.0: THE POWER OF FLEXIBLE WITHDRAWAL STRATEGIES

- Bengen's CIA
- three other inflation adjustment rules on their own
- the three advanced strategies combined with Bengen's CIA

The method

- I've modelled them all using and comparing historical data between 1900 and 2016, inclusive.
- I compare the three inflation-adjustment strategies with the baseline strategy, which is Bengen's CIA.
- Each retirement block lasts 30 years.
- The number of years of available data provided 87 separate scenarios but overlapping 30-year blocks of retirement.
- I work with a 50/50 UK Equity/UK Bond portfolio, with annual rebalancing.
- I give the gross safe withdrawal rate (ie no fees) and net safe withdrawal rate (ie net of 1% charges).

I've also selected some scenarios from the dataset and use them to illustrate the impact of inflation on the withdrawal during the retirement period.

- Cliff Edge Scenario: this is the 10th percentile historical scenario. Think of this as one of the very worst 30-year scenarios since 1900. The hypothetical retiree experienced very poor sequence of return and high inflation. Nine out of 10 historical scenarios were better than this.

- Comfy Scenario: this is the 50th percentile or median historical scenario, with relatively modest inflation and good sequence of return. Half of historical scenarios will be better than this.

- Cloud Nine: this is the 90th percentile historical scenario. This is one of the very best historical scenarios for retirees since 1900. Our hypothetical retiree enjoyed very good sequence of return and subdued inflation. Only one in 10 historical scenarios are better.

Inflation-adjustment withdrawal strategies

These strategies use different ways to adjust the withdrawals for inflation.

Fixed withdrawal – no inflation adjustment

A key feature of Bengen's SWR is that withdrawals are adjusted (up or down) for inflation every year. But there's abundant research to show that spending in retirement isn't static in real terms. In fact, spending tends to fall in real terms. Around 90% of annuities purchased are fixed annuities, without any index links or inflation adjustments.

So, what's the sustainable withdrawal rate if we don't adjust income for inflation?

The fixed or level withdrawal strategy defines withdrawal as a percentage of the initial portfolio. Subsequent amounts aren't adjusted for inflation. For instance, a withdrawal rate of 5% from a £100,000 portfolio will produce an income of £5,000 in the first year. The retiree takes an income of £5,000 each year. This happens regardless of the portfolio value and the income isn't adjusted for inflation. This strategy mimics level annuities.

Fig. 36 opposite compares fixed and inflation-adjusted withdrawals. It shows historical maximum sustainable withdrawal rates over a rolling 30-year period. A gross withdrawal rate of 4.5% (before fees) is the worst historical scenario for retirees opting for fixed withdrawals. This compares favourably with 3.1% for inflation-adjusted withdrawals.

Even after accounting for a 1% fee, the 50/50 UK portfolio still supports a fixed withdrawal of 4% of the initial portfolio over a 30-year period in the historical worst-case scenarios.

Most retirees appear to be comfortable with this approach, because they tend to spend progressively less as they get older.

However, with a fixed approach there's the danger that the real value of their income will fall faster than what they need. To understand the impact of inflation, we can compare the real income under this fixed withdrawal (FW) with Bengen's constant inflation-adjusted withdrawal (CIAW) strategy.

For this comparison, consider two hypothetical retirees, James and John. They each have a portfolio of £100,000. The asset allocation is the same 50/50 UK portfolio, with annual rebalancing and total portfolio charges of 1%. Our first retiree James adopts Bengen's CIAW method. He takes £2,600pa from his portfolio, which is then adjusted for inflation each year. Our second retiree John adopts the FW approach. He takes £3950pa from his portfolio but it's not adjusted for inflation in future years.

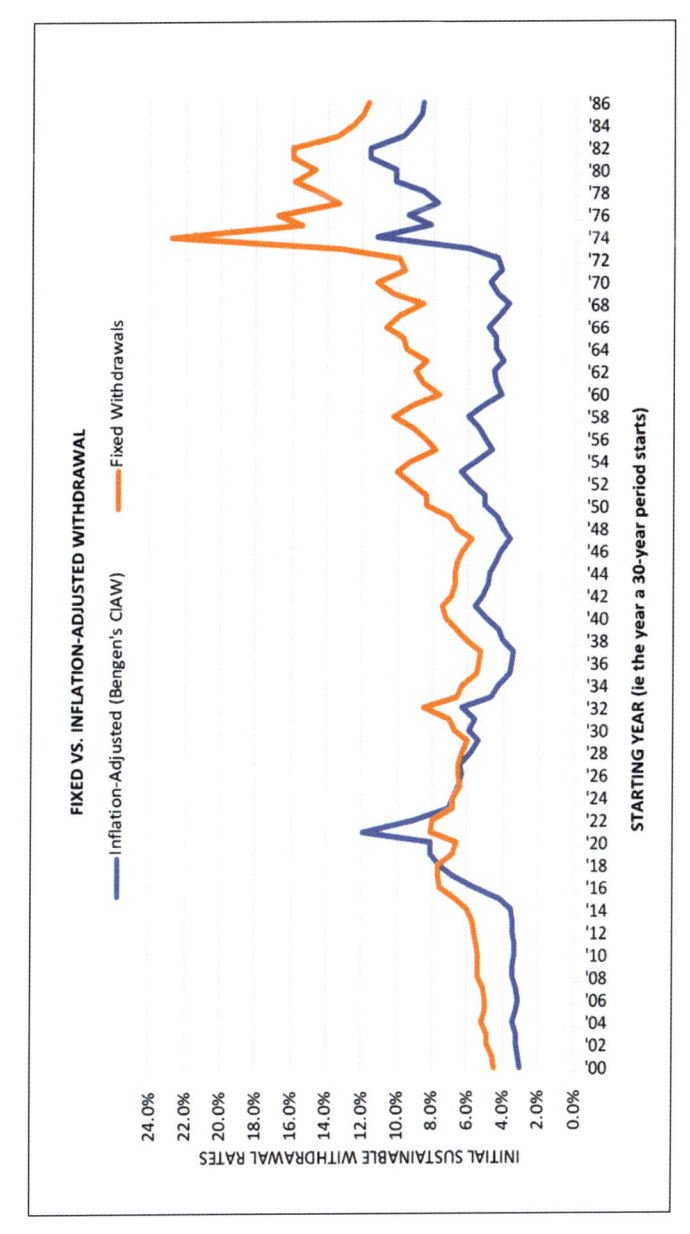

Fig. 36: Initial sustainable withdrawal rate: inflation-adjusted vs. fixed spending (no fee deducted)

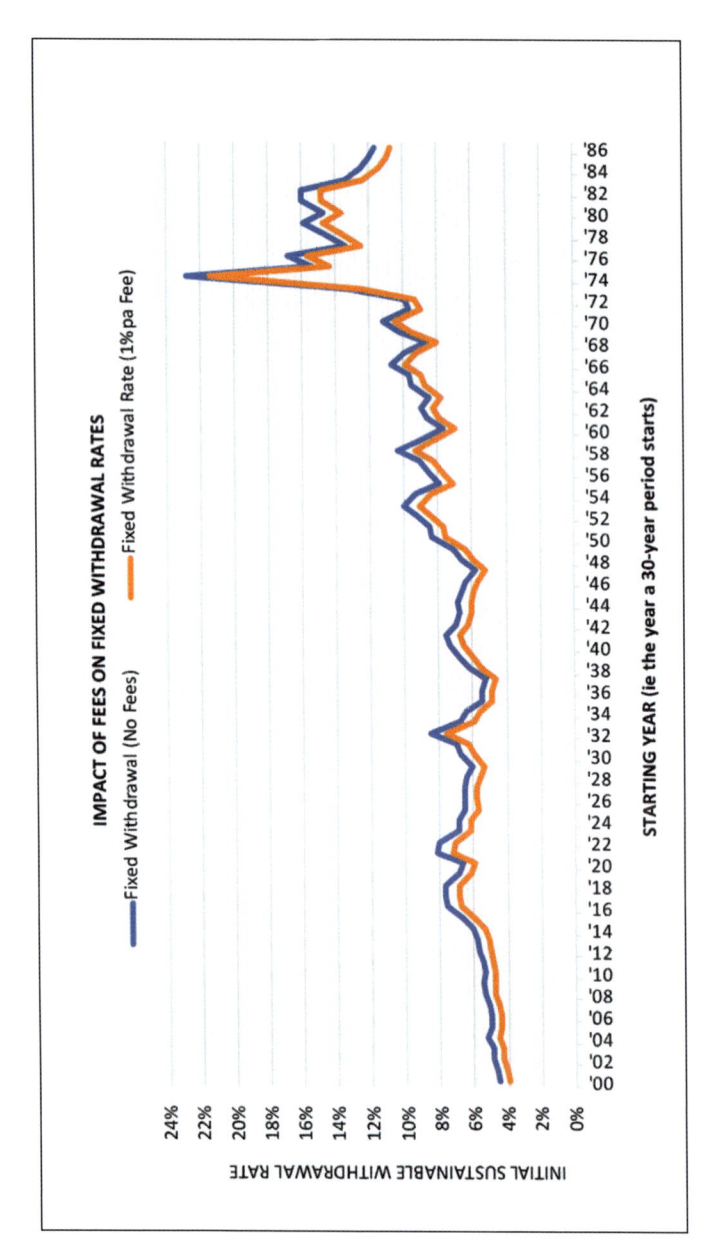

Fig. 37: Sustainable withdrawal rate: inflation-adjusted vs. fixed spending (1%pa fee deducted)

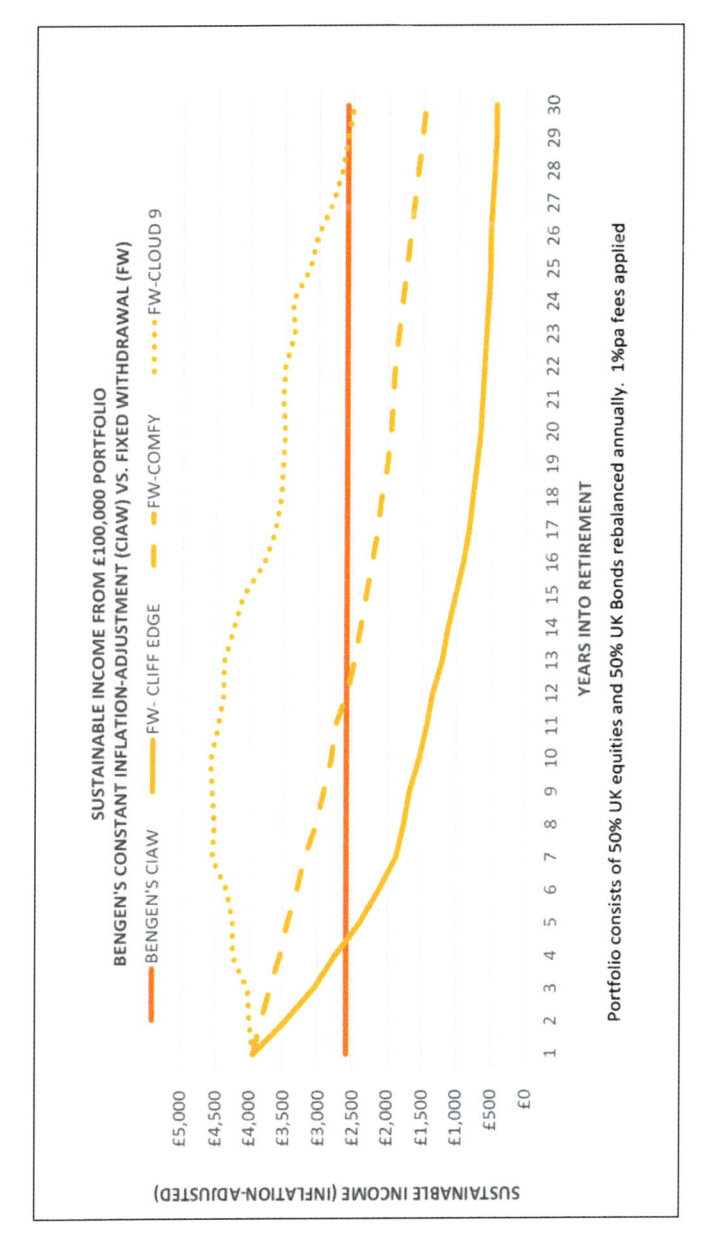

Fig. 38: Real income under Bengen's constant inflation-adjusted withdrawal vs. fixed withdrawal (1%pa fee deducted)

Fig. 38 compares income with Bengen's CIAW and the FW method in the three scenarios.

With Bengen's CIAW approach, the real income of £2,600pa is maintained under all the historical scenarios. So, we only see one glide path.

Under the FW approach, income starts at a much higher level of £4,000pa. But this declines rapidly under both the Cliff Edge (10th percentile) and Comfy (50th percentile) scenarios. These represent a decline of 73.62% and 40.98% respectively in real income by the 15th year of retirement. This is way more than the typical spending decline of 35% from age 65 to 80.

Over 90% of annuity purchases are level annuities rather than index-linked annuities. So, it appears many retirees are quite happy to tolerate inflation risk. This may be because the State Pension tends to keep up with or exceed inflation and it compensates for the decline in real income elsewhere.

So, if a client adopts the fixed percentage withdrawal, they can spend more in the early part of retirement, but the impact of inflation on their income may be too much for them.

Guyton inflation-adjustment withdrawal

The prospect of an income that falls progressively in real terms may not appear all that attractive to many retirees. And if investment returns turn out to be favourable (as you'd hope they would in the vast majority of circumstances), it would be nice to enjoy the upside.

One of the earliest proponents of rule-based spending is US-based financial planner Jonathan Guyton. His main point is that retirees don't want to play a game of chicken with their retirement portfolios and are often prepared to make compromises.

Guyton developed a set of rules and an approach to make sure withdrawals last a lifetime. These rules can be applied together, but they're also effective individually.

In this section, I want to model one of Guyton's individual rules. The rules state that: withdrawals are adjusted for inflation annually except in the years after a negative portfolio return.

This rule is a half-way house between Bengen's inflation-adjusted withdrawal and the fixed withdrawal.

Fig. 39 compares the historical withdrawal rates under the Guyton inflation adjustment (GIA), the fixed withdrawal and Bergen's CIAW.

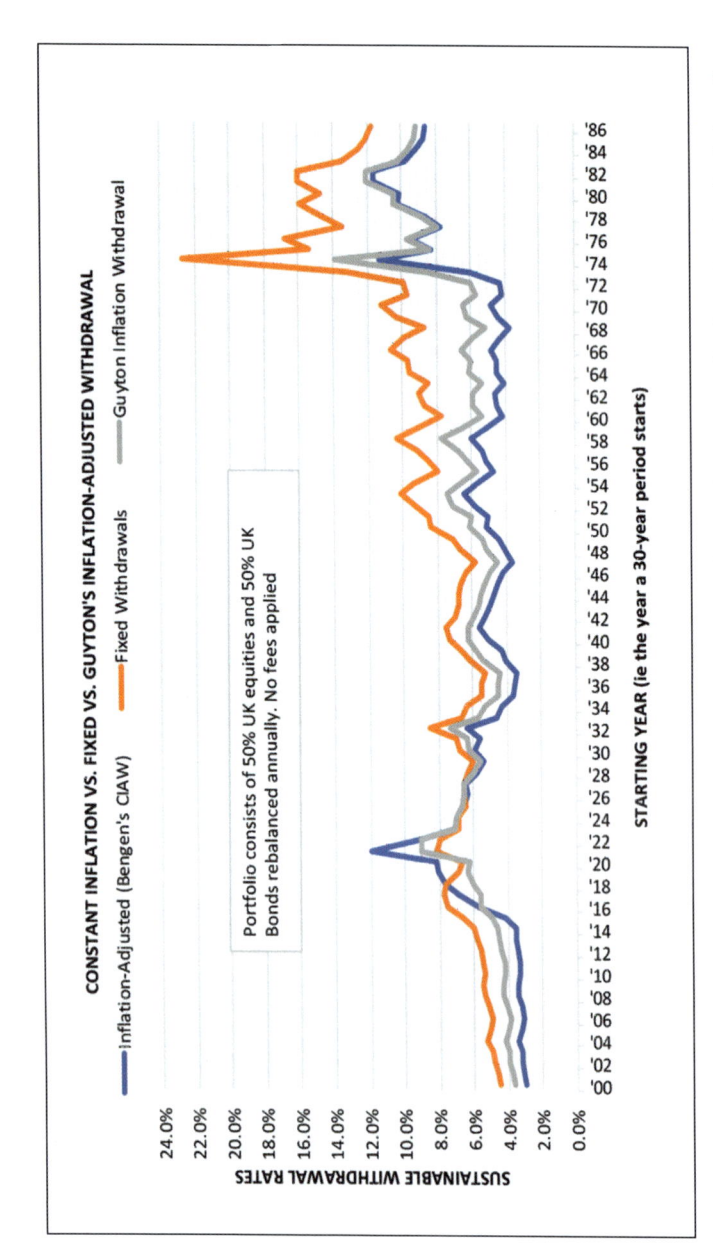

Fig. 39: Initial sustainable withdrawal rate: Inflation-adjusted vs. Guyton inflation adjustment vs. Fixed spending (no fee deducted)

A GIA strategy produces a sustainable withdrawal rate of 3.7%, compared to 3.1% for inflation-adjusted withdrawal and 4.5% for fixed withdrawal. This is before fees of course.

Even after we apply 1% for charges, SWR under the GIA strategy is still a tidy 3.2%, compared to 2.6% under Bengen's CIAW.

Again, in Fig. 40 we'll compare the spending glide path in real terms under both strategies using our three scenarios – Cliff Edge (10th percentile), Comfy (50th percentile) and Cloud Nine (90th percentile).

With the GIA approach, income starts at a higher level than Bengen's CIAW, at £3170pa. But it declines progressively under both the Cliff Edge (10th percentile) and Comfy (50th percentile) scenarios. These represent a decline of 38.62% and 16.09% respectively in real income by the 15th year in retirement. This is more in line with the typical spending decline of 35% from age 65 to 80.

By the 30th year in retirement, spending has declined by a total of 44.11% and 29.54% under the Cliff Edge and Comfy scenarios respectively.

The Guyton inflation-adjustment approach is much more in sync with a typical retirement spending pattern. It means you can start spending at a higher level than Bengen's CIAW, but the decline in real terms is much more constrained than the fixed withdrawal strategy.

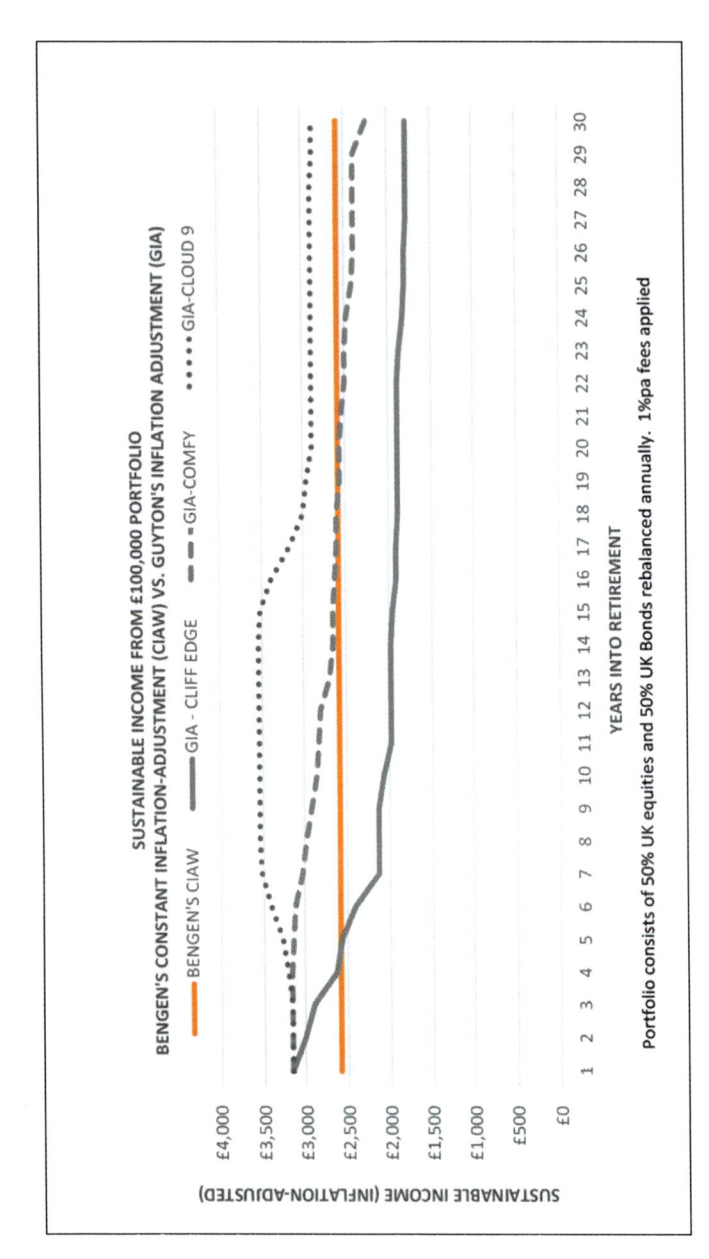

Fig. 40: Real income under Bengen's constant inflation-adjusted withdrawal vs. Guyton inflation adjustment (1%pa fee deducted)

Cap and collar inflation adjustment

This is another halfway house between constant inflation adjustment (CIAW) and fixed withdrawal (FW) strategies. The cap and collar inflation-adjustment approach addresses the problem of extreme inflation and deflation.

Under Bengen's rule, you adjust withdrawals for inflation, regardless. This includes historical periods of double-digit inflation, particularly between 1915-1920 and most of the 1970s.

There were also periods of deflation – for instance in 1921 when prices fell by over 20%. Retirees would have had to cut their withdrawals consecutively over a period of five years in the late 1920s. While the real spending power of each year's withdrawal remains the same, it could be a challenge explaining this to the client. These extremes are a key reason why Bengen's SWR for the UK is so low in the early 1900s.

A rule-based approach could be used to cap and collar each year's inflation adjustments. This way, retirees can avoid extreme changes to their income withdrawal, at least in a nominal sense. A cap-and-collar approach also matches the typical retirement spending pattern. Income increases in real terms but at a slower pace than inflation.

Here I've applied a cap of 5% to inflation and a collar of 0%. (Advisers can model any combination of cap and collar through Timelineapp.co.)

Fig. 41 shows the Cap and Collar 5/0 approach gives very similar withdrawal rates to Bengen's CIAW: a SWR of 3.6%, compared to 3.1% under Bengen's CIAW and 3.7% under the GIAW, before charges.

After applying a 1% fee, the cap and collar 5/0 (CC) produced a net sustainable withdrawal rate of 3.1%, compared to 2.6% under Bengen's CIAW.

With the CC, income starts at a higher level than Bengen's CIAW - £3120pa - and it's maintained under the Cloud Nine scenario.

Under the Cliff Edge (10th percentile) and Comfy (50th percentile) scenarios, real income declines progressively by 50.25% and 9.5% respectively. This decline under the Cliff Edge scenario is higher than the typical spending decline of 35% from age 65 to 80.

By the 30th year, real income has declined by about 60.9%.

My view is that the cap and collar strategy works well under most scenarios, with low or even moderate inflation. But, if inflation constantly exceeds the cap, then real spending is decimated.

For the cap and collar strategy, by the 15th year of retirement, the real income has declined by 38.62% and 16.09% respectively under the Cliff Edge and Comfy scenarios. This is in line with the spending decline of 35%

CAP AND COLLAR INFLATION ADJUSTMENT

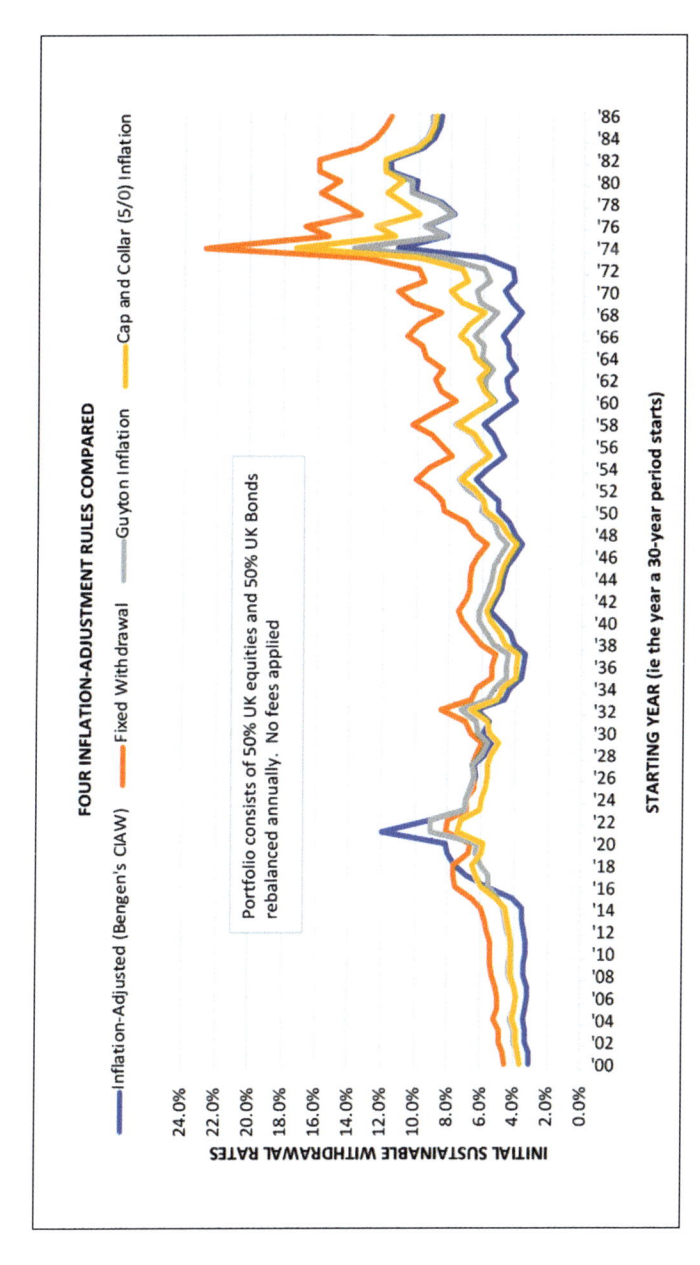

Fig. 41: Initial sustainable withdrawal rate under four inflation-adjustement rules compared

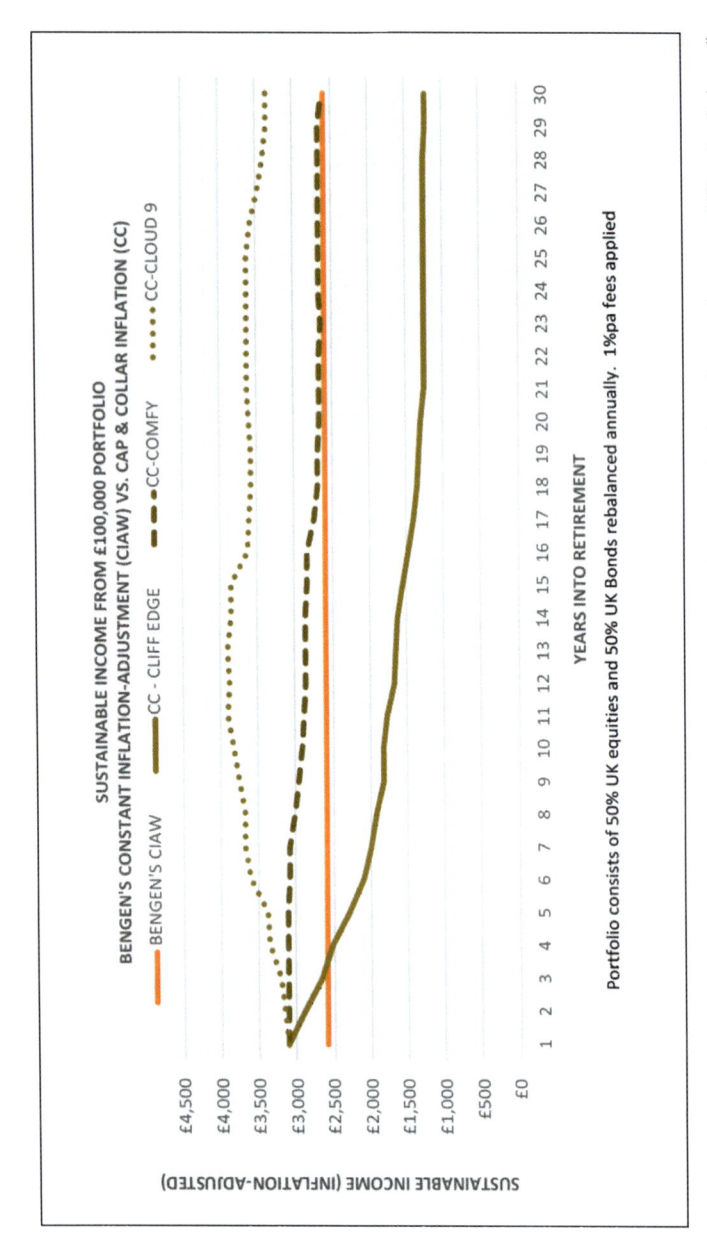

Fig. 42: Real income under Bengen's constant inflation-adjusted withdrawal vs. cap and collar inflation adjustment (1%pa fee deducted)

of an average retiree, from age 65 to 80. By the 30th year in retirement, spending has declined by a total of **44.11%** and **29.54%** under the Cliff Edge and Comfy scenarios, respectively.

Advanced withdrawal strategies

The advanced withdrawal strategies make further adjustments to the withdrawal over and above inflation adjustments. In practice, there are 12 possible strategies. You can combine the advanced withdrawals with any of the four inflation-adjustment rules discussed in the earlier section.

But, for the sake of simplicity, I've adopted Bengen's CIAW rule for all three advanced withdrawal strategies.

Guardrail strategy

Financial planner Jonathan Guyton designed the original guardrail strategies. He discussed them in his article[22] in the October 2004 edition of the Journal of Financial Planning.

He later refined them and discussed this in a second article[23] published with co-author William Klinger. The rules allow higher withdrawal rates. But, future spending won't always increase with inflation each year and retirees may need to cut their spending in certain circumstances. The approach is designed to make sure withdrawal is sustainable over a much longer period of 40 years. Typically, one or more of four decision rules are applied to a retiree's portfolio.

Guyton and Klinger's four decision rules can be implemented individually or combined.

- The portfolio management rule: take the gains from an asset class that's performed best in the previous year to provide the income. Move excess portfolio gains (beyond what's needed for the withdrawal) into a cash account to fund future withdrawals.

---

22 Guyton, Jonathan T. "Decision Rules and Portfolio Management for Retirees: Is the 'Safe' Initial Withdrawal Rate Too Safe?" Journal of Financial Planning October 2004: 54–62.

23 Guyton, Jonathan T., & Klinger, William J. "Decision Rules and Maximum Initial Withdrawal Rates". Journal of Financial Planning, March 2006.

- Inflation-adjustment rule (also known as the withdrawal rule): increase withdrawal in line with inflation unless the previous year's portfolio total return was negative. Withdrawals are frozen in the years following a negative portfolio return to minimise the danger of pound-cost ravaging.

- The capital preservation rule: if the current withdrawal rate rises above 20% of the initial rate, then current spending is reduced by 10%.

- The prosperity rule: spending in the current year is raised by 10% if the current withdrawal rate has fallen by more than 20% below the initial withdrawal rate.

The authors described the capital preservation and prosperity rules as the guardrails. This is because these rules govern withdrawals under both negative and positive extreme conditions. Unless conditions are extreme (the current year's withdrawal rate straying more than 20% from the initial withdrawal rate), the portfolio and withdrawal rules are enough to govern withdrawals.

Under the inflation-adjustment strategies, we examined the impact of implementing Guyton's inflation-adjustment rule individually. In this section, I examine the impact of implementing the guardrail strategy – ie a combination of the capital preservation and prosperity rules – as well as the inflation rule.

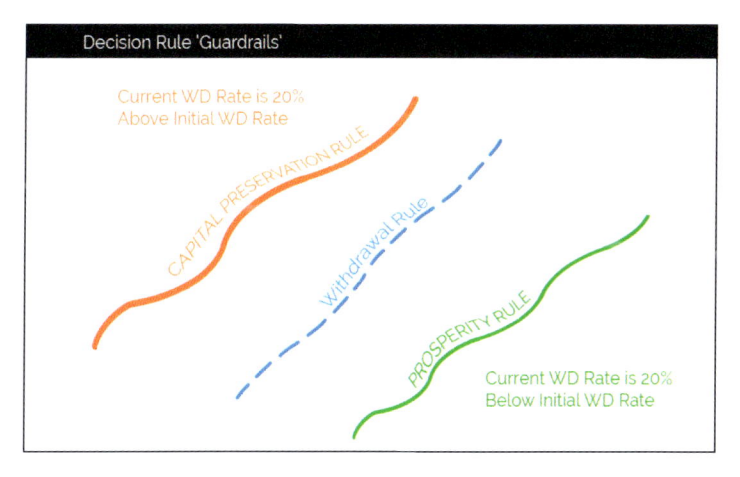

Fig. 43: Guyton's Guardrails

The guardrail strategy simply makes sure that withdrawal doesn't become so high that it decimates the portfolio beyond a point of no return. For example, you reduce spending by 10% if the current withdrawal rate goes above 20% of the initial withdrawal rate. Conversely, you raise spending in the current year by 10% if the current withdrawal rate has fallen by more than 20% below the initial withdrawal rate.

I've used the 20% guardrail and 10% income adjustment in my model, but advisers can choose whatever guardrail figures they prefer. You can read an in-depth discussion by Klinger in this article.[24]

---

24 Klinger, William J. 2016. "Guardrails to Prevent Potential Retirement Portfolio Failure." Journal of Financial Planning 29 (10): 46–53.

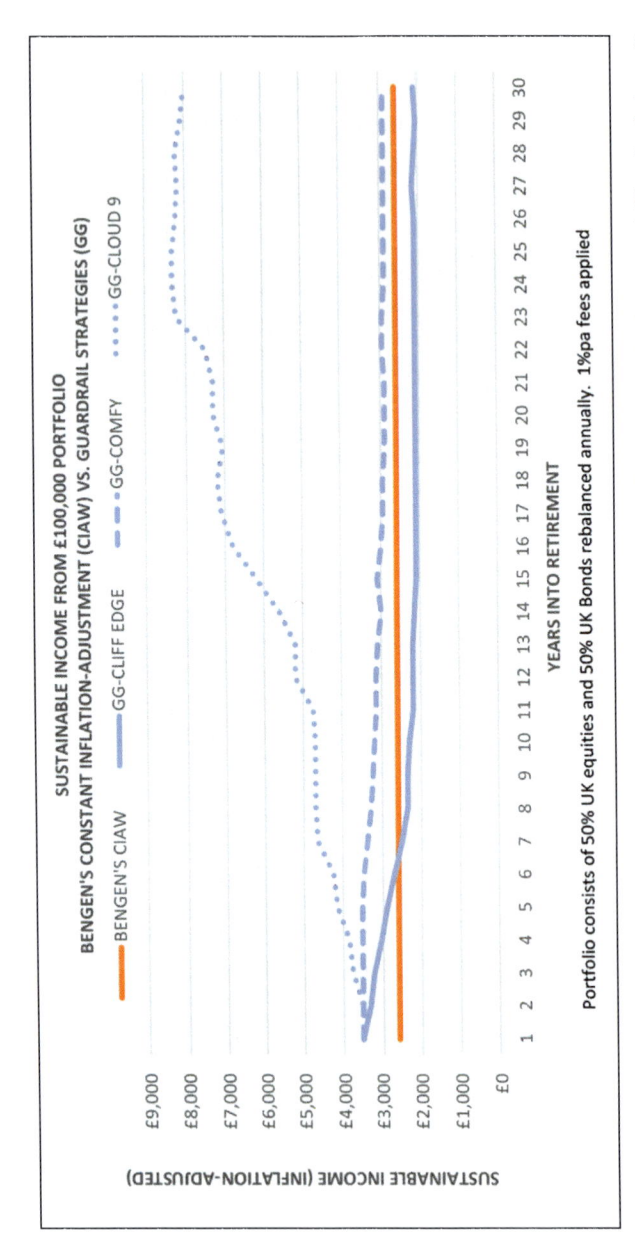

Fig. 44: Real income under Bengen's constant inflation-adjusted withdrawal vs. Guyton's guardrails strategy (1%pa fee deducted)

When I tested the Guyton guardrail strategy through UK periods between 1900 to 2016, it produced a net initial withdrawal rate of 3.5%, assuming a 1% fee. This compares favourably with Bengen's baseline rate of 2.6%.

Under the Cliff Edge (10th percentile) and Comfy (50th percentile) scenarios, real income declines progressively by 40.38% and 11.54%, respectively. This decline under the Cliff Edge scenario is slightly higher than the typical spending decline of 35% from age 65 to 80.

One key advantage of the guardrail strategy is that it naturally allows significantly more spending under the Cloud Nine scenario, with real income rising by over 75% at the 15th year.

So, is there any significant advantage in applying the guardrail strategy over and above the simple Guyton inflation adjustment? Definitely. Retirees are more likely to experience a better sequence of return than the historical worst-case scenario, so the guardrail strategy means they can enjoy more upside under most market conditions.

Ratcheting strategy

This strategy was first described by financial planner Michael Kitces in his 2015 article[25]. Kitces's main point is that Bengen's baseline 4% rule is too conservative. This is because it's based on the worst historical sequence of return. In reality, an overwhelming majority of market scenarios would support a higher withdrawal rate. So, Kitces proposed that a retiree starts out with the baseline withdrawal rate, but can increase their spending by 10% if the portfolio value exceeds 150% of the original value. There's a caveat: these spending increases can only take place once every three years at most.

His rationale for this is very simple: *'if the portfolio gets "far enough" ahead, spending can be increased – but not increased so quickly that the retiree might have to go backwards shortly thereafter.'* Of course, retirees experiencing a favourable sequence of returns will inevitably sit down for a portfolio/retirement review. They'll realise they're so far ahead that it's safe to increase spending anyway.

This ratcheting strategy is a particularly good approach to tackling sequence risk. Since the first 10 years in retirement are crucial, if the client experiences a good start, then they can increase withdrawal. The strategy is most effective if the initial withdrawal rate is conservative in the first place. This

---

25 The Ratcheting Safe Withdrawal Rate – A More Dominant Version Of The 4% Rule? https://www.kitces.com/blog/the-ratcheting-safe-withdrawal-rate-a-more-dominant-version-of-the-4-rule/

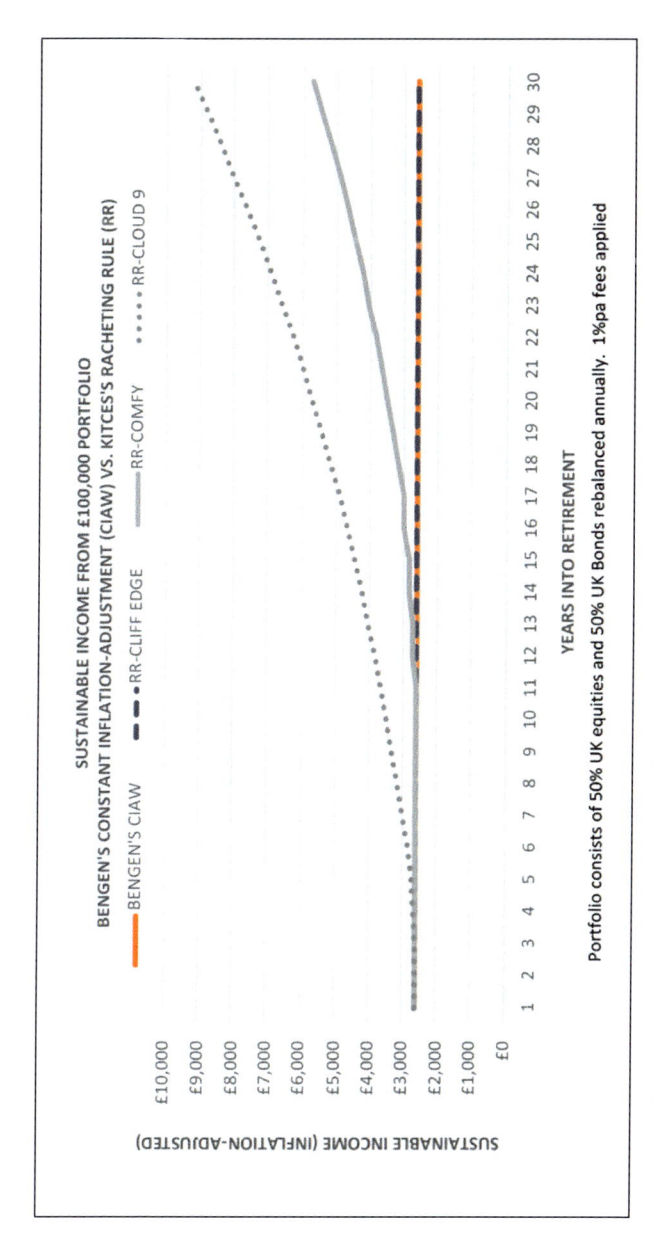

Fig. 45: Real income under Bengen's constant inflation-adjusted withdrawal vs. Kitces's ratcheting rule (1%pa fee deducted)

is an opposite approach to the guardrail strategy, which aims to starts with higher spending that reduces if there's a poor sequence of return.

The downside is that the ratcheting approach may go against the consumption pattern of most retirees, where spending tends to start higher and then reduces progressively in the later part of retirement. I've tested the ratcheting rule and concluded that a more conservative increase of 5% (rather than the 10% proposed by Kitces) is more appropriate if the portfolio value exceeds 150% of the original value.

Floor and ceiling strategy

This method was put forward by William Bengen in a 2001 article in the Journal of Financial Planning[26]. The strategy allows a retiree to withdraw a percentage of their outstanding portfolio each year. But it's subject to defined minimum and maximum amounts based on the income in the first year of retirement.

The rationale is that withdrawing a percentage of your outstanding portfolio each year results in too many fluctuations in income and makes budgeting particularly hard. By adding a floor and a ceiling in monetary terms, you're assured that income won't fall below a given minimum.

Overall, the strategy allows greater spending when markets are up and lower spending when markets are down – subject to the floor and ceiling – in real terms.

Bengen originally proposed a ceiling of 20% above the first year of retirement income and a floor of 15% of the same. You adjust the floor and ceiling for inflation.

Retirees can set their own floor and ceiling, depending on the level of modification to their income they're prepared to accept.

---

26 Bengen, William P. (2001): Conserving Client Portfolios During Retirement, Part IV. Journal of Financial Planning; May2001, Vol. 14 Issue 5, p110

Flexible spending strategies compared

Having looked at these strategies, let's compare all six withdrawal strategies with the baseline (Bergen's CIA withdrawal) scenarios.

Figs. 47-49 below show the initial SWR for a £100,000 portfolio and the inflation-adjusted income in the first, 15th and 30th years of retirement for all the withdrawal strategies. The scenarios are the 10th percentile (Cliff Edge), 50th percentile (Comfy) and 90th percentile (Cloud Nine) of all historical 30-year periods between 1900 and 2015.

Figs. 50-52 show the real income for all the withdrawal strategies under the three scenarios.

The main conclusion is that Guyton inflation-adjustment and guardrail rules delivered spending experiences that are most consistent with a retiree's likely spending pattern in retirement. These strategies let retirees enjoy higher income in the early part of their retirement. If they encounter a Cliff Edge market scenario, their withdrawal gradually declines in line with their consumption pattern. If they experience good scenarios (Comfy), then their withdrawal declines but at a much slower pace than their consumption pattern.

Of course, if they experience a Cloud Nine type of market scenario (which is unlikely), their withdrawal will increase drastically while their consumption pattern declines. This is

FLEXIBLE SPENDING STRATEGIES COMPARED

	£100,000 initial pot invested in 50/50 equity/bond portfolio, rebalanced annually						
	Withdrawal strategies	Net SWR	1st Yr. income	15th Yr. income	30th Yr. income	% Change by 15th yr.	% Change by 30th yr.
Baseline	Bengen's constant inflation adjustment	2.60%	£2,600	£2,600	£2,600	0%	0%
Inflation adjustment	Fixed withdrawal	4.00%	£3,950	£1,042	£449	-73.60%	-88.60%
	Guyton inflation adjustment	3.20%	£3,170	£1,946	£1,772	-38.60%	-44.10%
	Cap and collar inflation adjustment	3.10%	£3,120	£1,552	£1,220	-50.30%	-60.90%
Advanced withdrawal rules	Guardrails strategy	3.50%	£3,500	£2,087	£2,092	-40.40%	-40.20%
	Ratcheting strategy	2.60%	£2,600	£2,600	£2,600	0.00%	0.00%
	Floor & ceiling strategy	2.60%	£2,600	£2,600	£2,600	0.00%	0.00%

Fig. 46: SWR (net of 1%pa charge) for variable withdrawal strategies (Cliff Edge scenario)

	£100,000 initial pot invested in 50/50 equity/bond portfolio, rebalanced annually						
	Withdrawal strategies	Net SWR	1st Yr. income	15th Yr. income	30th Yr. income	% Change by 15th yr.	% Change by 30th yr.
Baseline	Bengen's constant inflation adjustment	2.60%	£2,600	£2,600	£2,600	0%	0%
Inflation adjustment	Fixed withdrawal	4.00%	£3,950	£2,331	£1,468	-40.90%	-62.80%
	Guyton inflation adjustment	3.20%	£3,170	£2,660	£2,233	-16.10%	-29.60%
	Cap and collar inflation adjustment	3.10%	£3,120	£2,825	£2,617	-9.40%	-16.10%
Advanced withdrawal rules	Guardrails strategy	3.50%	£3,500	£3,096	£2,874	-11.50%	-17.90%
	Ratcheting strategy	2.60%	£2,600	£2,867	£5,675	10.30%	118.30%
	Floor & ceiling strategy	2.60%	£2,600	£2,600	£2,600	0.00%	0.00%

Fig. 47: SWR (net of %pa charge) for variable withdrawal strategies (Comfy scenario)

	£100,000 initial pot invested in 50/50 equity/bond portfolio, rebalanced annually						
	Withdrawal strategies	Net SWR	1st Yr. income	15th Yr. income	30th Yr. income	% Change by 15th yr.	% Change by 30th yr.
Baseline	Bengen's constant inflation adjustment	2.60%	£2,600	£2,600	£2,600	0%	0%
Inflation adjustment	Fixed withdrawal	4.00%	£3,950	£4,107	£2,508	3.90%	-36.50%
	Guyton inflation adjustment	3.20%	£3,170	£3,518	£2,868	10.90%	-9.50%
	Cap and collar inflation adjustment	3.10%	£3,120	£3,839	£3,346	23.00%	7.20%
Advanced withdrawal rules	Guardrails strategy	3.50%	£3,500	£6,179	£7,970	76.50%	127.70%
	Ratcheting strategy	2.60%	£2,600	£4,447	£9,245	71.00%	255.50%
	Floor & ceiling strategy	2.60%	£2,600	£2,600	£2,600	0.00%	0.00%

Fig. 48: SWR (net of 1%pa charge) for variable withdrawal strategies (Cloud Nine scenario)

a nice problem to have! The guardrail lets them enjoy some of their upside while they can, without putting their future spending at risk.

Sustainable income (net of 1%pa charge) for various withdrawal strategies[27]

The Kitces ratcheting rule and Bergen's floor and ceiling don't offer any improvement in the initial SWR under both the Cliff Edge and Comfy scenarios. Withdrawals are pretty much in line with the baseline strategy. If retirees encounter a Cloud Nine type scenario, then the ratcheting rule makes sure they don't die with too much money in the bank!

Overall, I believe the Guyton strategy (inflation-adjustment and the guardrail) is a superior approach. This is because the spending pattern is more consistent with a typical retirement spending pattern. Retirees can spend more in the earlier part of retirement and reduce the amount gradually, without a sudden shock if they encounter a poor sequence of returns.

---

27 Under the Cliff Edge Scenario, the Floor & Ceiling and Ratcheting Rule essentially follow the same path as the Baseline strategy, which is why they don't show up on the chart. The Ratcheting Rule diverges under the Comfy and Cloud Nine scenarios.

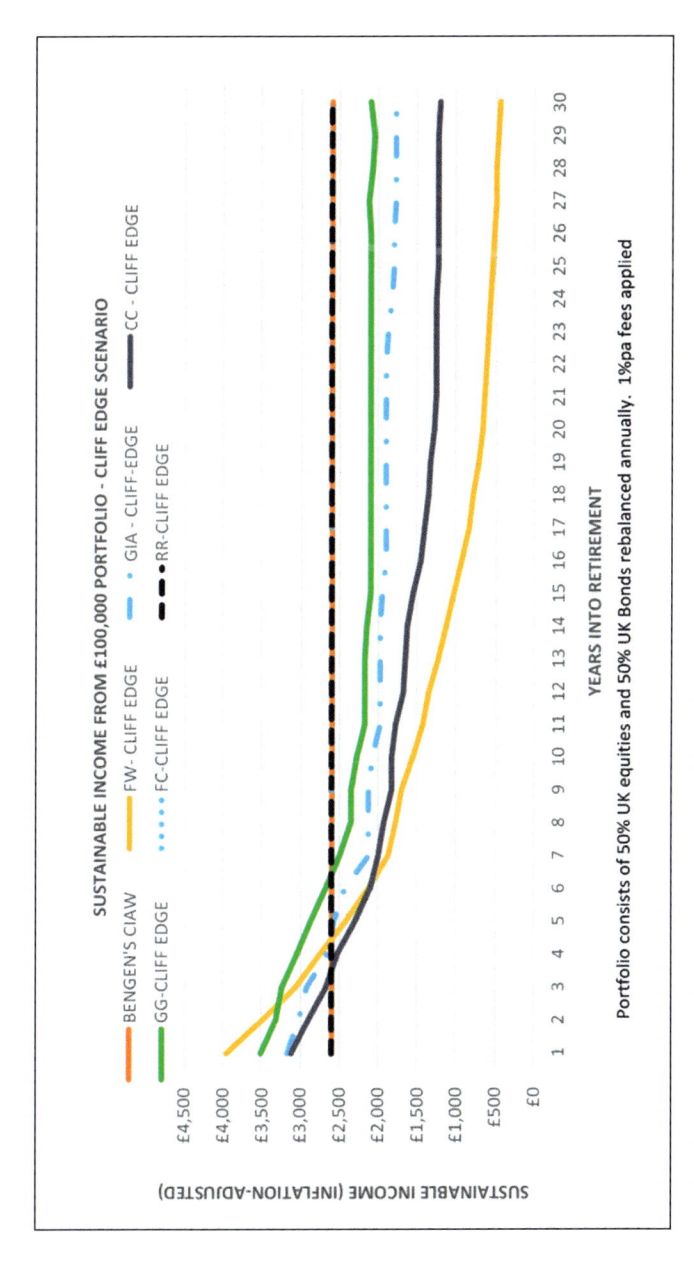

Fig. 49: Real income under various withdrawal (Cliff Edge scenario)

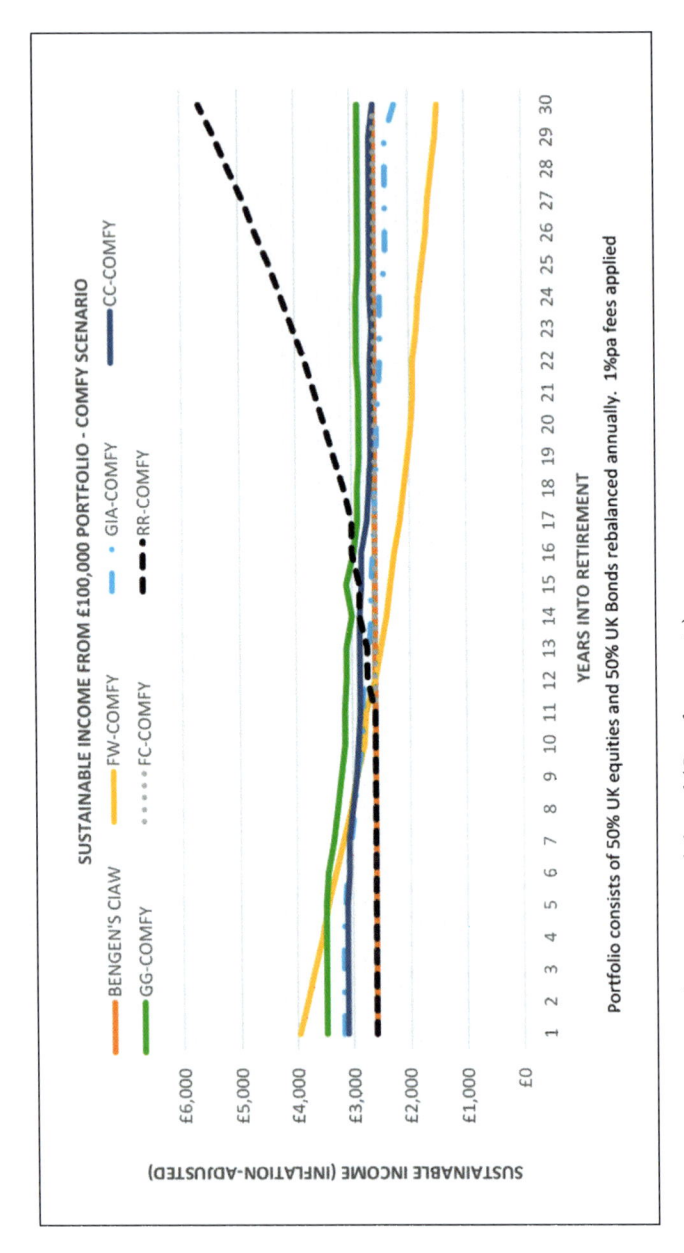

Fig. 50: Real income under various withdrawal (Comfy scenario)

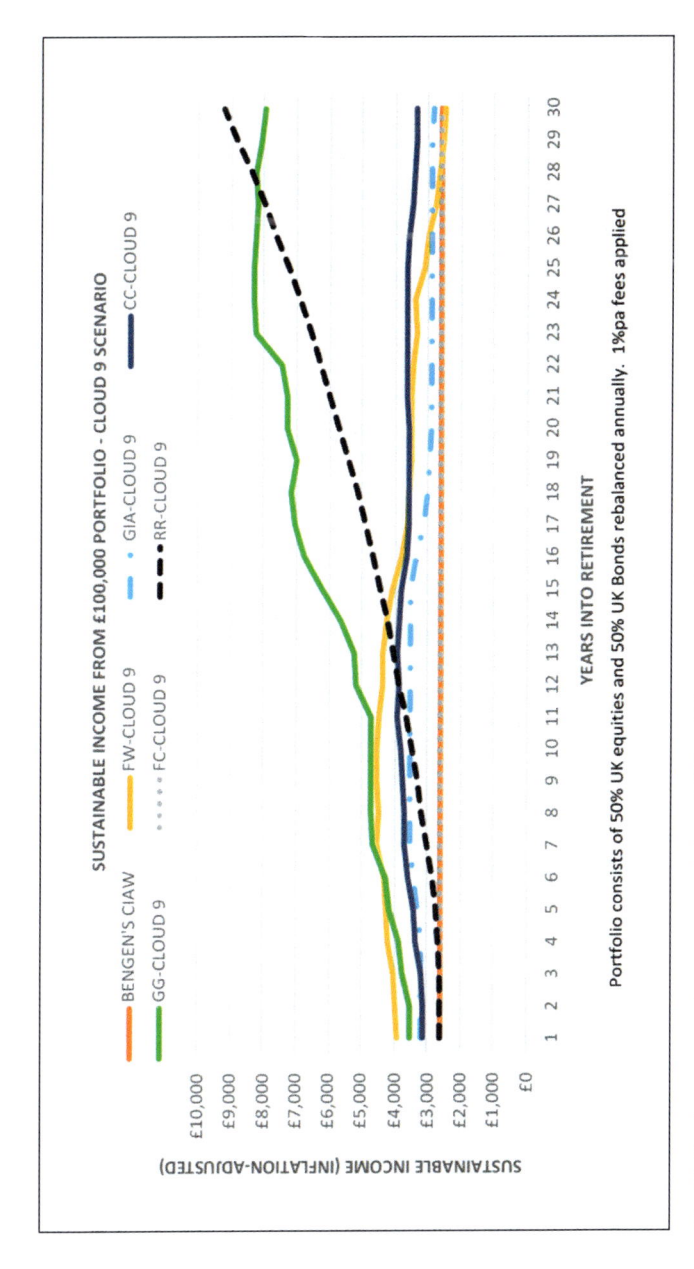

Fig. 51: Real income under various withdrawal (Cloud Nine scenario)

Adjusting sustainable withdrawal for different phases of retirement

Another way to modify portfolio withdrawal is to consider the effect of scaling income up or down at different stages of retirement.

As I mentioned, research in the UK shows retirement spending declines progressively in real terms. It's typically about 35% lower at age 80 than it was at age 65.

Real spending tends to decline a little at the beginning of retirement, accelerates its decline in the middle, and then slows its decline again in the final decade. Researchers identified three unique phases of retirement dubbed:

- the Go-Go years, the active first decade of retirement
- the Slow-Go years, the less-active second decade of retirement
- the No-Go years, the final decade of retirement when most discretionary spending stops

An ideal withdrawal strategy should take account of this. Retirees should be able to spend more in their Go-Go years when they're more active. It's done in the knowledge that they'll scale down their income later on when they're less active.

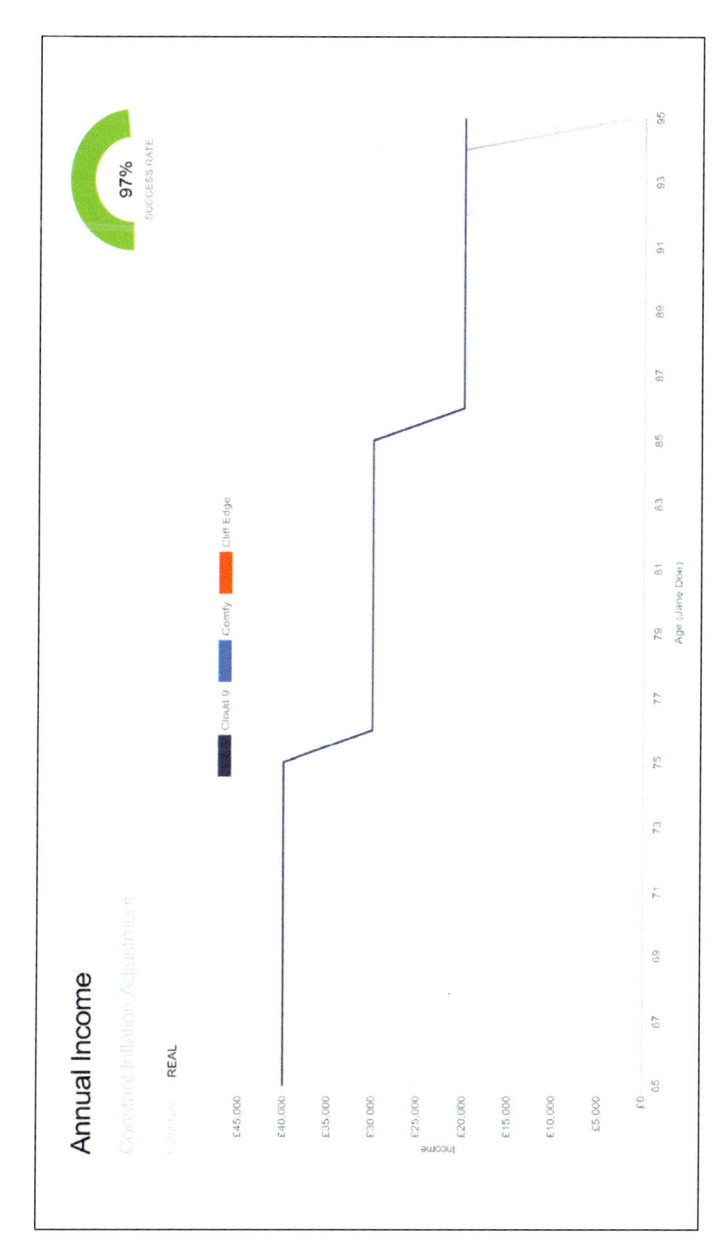

Fig. 52: Real income with three phases of retirement

For instance, you can illustrate a scenario where the client with £1m invested in a 50/50 UK equity/bond portfolio withdraws:

- £40,000 each year from age 65 to 75
- £30,000 each year from age 76 to 85
- £20,000 each year from then

Fig. 52 shows the real (inflation-adjusted) withdrawal for all rolling 30-year periods between 1900 and 2016.

We can be more deliberate about the withdrawal strategy for each retiree if we take account of these types of lifestyle changes. Illustrations like this can also help retirees better prepare for likely changes to their income. It'll ultimately extend the longevity of their portfolio.

Of course, each person is different and it's impossible to predict the exact pattern of change. However, our planning is based on best guess, which is informed by empirical data on current retirees.

The power of one-degree course correction

In 1979 a passenger jet with 257 people on board left New Zealand for a sightseeing flight to Antarctica and back. Unknown to the pilots, someone had modified the flight coordinates by a mere two degrees. This error placed the aircraft 28 miles (45km) to the east of where the pilots assumed they were. As they approached Antarctica, the pilots descended to a lower altitude to give passengers a better look at the landscape. Although both were experienced pilots, neither had made this particular flight before, and they had no way of knowing that the incorrect coordinates had placed them directly in the path of Mount Erebus, an active volcano that rises from the frozen landscape to a height of more than 12,000 feet (3,700 m).

As the pilots flew onward, the white of the snow and ice covering the volcano blended with the white of the clouds above, making it appear as though they were flying over flat ground. By the time the instruments sounded the warning that the ground was rising fast towards them, it was too late. The aeroplane crashed into the side of the volcano, killing everyone on board.

It was a terrible tragedy caused by a minor error—a matter of only a few degrees[28].

---

28 See Uchtdorf D., (2008): A Matter of a Few Degrees https://www.lds.org/general-conference/2008/04/a-matter-of-a-few-degrees?lang=eng&_r=1 and full story in Arthur Marcel (2007): "Mount Erebus Plane Crash," www.abc.net.au/rn/ockhamsrazor/stories/2007/1814952.htm

Experts in air navigation have a rule of thumb known as the one-in-60 rule. It states that for every one degree a plane veers off its course, you'll miss your target by one mile for every 60 miles you fly. And more importantly, the further you travel, the further you are from your destination. If you veer off course by one degree, flying around the equator will land you almost 500 miles off target!

The point here is that managing a withdrawal strategy in drawdown isn't a set-and-forget approach. The flexible withdrawal strategies illustrate exactly this point, despite what some people incorrectly believe. It's crucial to review the plan regularly and make course corrections where necessary.

CHAPTER 7

Estimating probability of success

'I know of no way of judging the future but by the past'

– Patrick Henry

So far, we've defined the sustainable withdrawal rate and looked at several sustainable withdrawal strategies. The SWR framework assumes market conditions are going to be as bad as they've ever been. As the saying goes, plan for the worst, hope for the best.

But if we consider that the vast majority of market conditions are likely to be better than the historical worst case, could retirees enjoy a higher withdrawal rate? Perhaps a rate that's succeeded nine out of 10 times? And, since this is a 30-year journey or more for most clients, we can make adjustments along the way if things do turn out worse than we expect.

An advantage of understanding sequence risk is that a retiree can judge their first few years in retirement against other historical periods. It then becomes clearer whether they're heading for a retirement that's likely to be better or worse than during these other historical periods. They can then adjust their plan if they need to.

So, we don't necessarily have to base the sustainable withdrawal rate on the absolute historical worst-case scenario. We can bring in the concept of probability of success (PoS or success rate) or the probability of failure (PoF or failure rate).

- Success rate: this shows the percentage of times that a given withdrawal rate has lasted the full retirement period. There are 86 rolling 30-year periods between 1900 and 2015. A net withdrawal rate of 3% (net of 1%) has lasted at 30 years in 71 out of 86 historical periods, giving a success rate of 82.6% (ie 71/86 X 100).

- Failure rate: this shows the opposite. It's the percentage of times that the portfolio has run out before the end of the period, with a given withdrawal rate. So, the portfolio ran out within 30 years in 15 out of the 86 rolling 30-year periods when it used a net withdrawal of 3%. This is a PoF of 17.4% (100% - 82.6%).

We can illustrate success rate with extensive historical data or Monte Carlo simulation. Historical data over 100 years provides a colourful perspective of how a retirement plan would have fared under a wide range of market conditions. Monte Carlo simulations generate more random – but probable – scenarios.

Why probability?

Defining one's retirement strategy in terms of probability of success or failure may seem odd at first. Some financial professionals (in particular, those who subscribe to the safety-first school of thought) push back against the concept of probability. But it just acknowledges that there's always a risk associated with any retirement plan.

The concept of probability is used in many other fields, including medicine – particularly surgery, where lives may be at risk. Compare this with retirement, where one's money (and lifestyle) is at risk. Arguably, if it's good enough for medicine, it's good enough for retirement planning.

In his book, *Against the Gods*, Peter Bernstein highlights the crucial role of probability in modern-day risk management in many fields. He notes that[29], *'Without a command of probability theory and other instruments of risk management, engineers could never have designed the great bridges that span our widest rivers, homes would still be heated by fireplaces or parlor stoves, electric power utilities would not exist, polio would still be maiming children, no airplanes would fly, and space travel would be just a dream.'*

He goes on to say,

---

29 Bernstein, Peter L.. Against the Gods: The Remarkable Story of Risk (Kindle Locations 172-174). Wiley. Kindle Edition.

'As the years passed, mathematicians transformed probability theory from a gamblers' toy into a powerful instrument for organizing, interpreting, and applying information. As one ingenious idea was piled on top of another, quantitative techniques of risk management emerged that have helped trigger the tempo of modern times.'

Bernstein concludes that,

'Without numbers, there are no odds and no probabilities; without odds and probabilities, the only way to deal with risk is to appeal to the gods and the fates. Without numbers, risk is wholly a matter of gut[30].'

The point here is that probability theory is a well-established and powerful way to quantify and manage risk.

It's important to understand the difference between probability and prediction. Probability estimates the chances of an event, based on previously observed behaviour. Prediction, on the other hand, is a futile exercise.

Charlie Bilello, Director of Research at Pension Partners, LLC, sums it up rather nicely. *'The difference between a prediction and a probability is the difference between a pundit and a professional. One makes concentrated bets on the belief that they can predict the future and the other diversifies with the understanding that they cannot.'*

---

30 Bernstein, Peter L. Against the Gods: The Remarkable Story of Risk (Kindle Locations 537-539). Wiley. Kindle Edition.

Estimating probability – where do you draw the line?

'Plans are useless. Planning is indispensable.'

– President Dwight D. Eisenhower

Estimating the probability of success of a retirement plan is just an attempt to quantify risk and prepare for it. Think of PoS as probability of staying on track, and PoF as probability of adjustment.

As my friend and legendary financial planner Michael Kitces notes, using a Monte Carlo model helps planners to *'quantify how often the future scenarios are likely to turn out to be problematic. We might run 10,000 future scenarios, find that 9,500 of them succeed and 500 of them fall short and quantify the results as a "95% probability of success" in achieving the goal. Yet rarely does anyone in "the other 5%" of scenarios actually just keep on spending under the original plan until one day he/she wakes up broke and all the checks are bouncing. Instead, at some point, an adjustment occurs to get back on track. Of course, the later the adjustment occurs, the more significant it may have to be in order to get back on track. But ultimately, most probabilities of "failure" are really just probabilities of needing to make an adjustment to get back on track*[31]*.'*

---

31 Kitces., M (2015) Is Financial Planning Software Incapable Of Formulating An Actual Financial Plan? Nerd's Eye View. https://www.kitces.com/blog/is-financial-planning-software-incapable-of-formulating-an-actual-financial-plan/

My view is that working to an overall probability of success of 80%-90% or more is reasonable in retirement income planning. This means that there's a 10%-20% chance you'll have to make an unplanned adjustment to a client's withdrawal plan if they experience poor returns in the early part of their retirement.

The key here is that you need to monitor sequence risk closely. Kitces sums this up rather nicely, *'In the military context, battle plans are recognised as essential. And this is true despite the famous saying that "no battle plan ever survives contact with the enemy" because the process of engaging the plan, progressing towards the goals, and seeing what happens once the enemy is engaged, will itself change and alter what the next step should be. Notwithstanding this challenge, the military engages in planning because it's only by trying to consider what the plan should be, and how it might be impacted by future events, that contingency plans can be created to know how to handle "unexpected" problems that arise.'*

In a sense, retirement income plans should be viewed as battle plans. When plans meet the real world, the real world doesn't yield to your plan. You must adapt whatever you're doing to reality.

Have a contingency?

As the saying goes, everybody has a plan until they get punched in the face!

It's crucial to consider the probability of success or failure of a withdrawal strategy as well as how long the pot would last under severe market conditions. It's just as important to have your contingency plan in place. For example, does the client have other assets like the family property that they can rely on if the worst-case scenario happens? Perhaps extreme longevity and poor sequence of return?

It's important that each retiree is comfortable with the probability of success. They should perhaps start with a much lower withdrawal rate or adopt a safety-first approach if they can't accept a 10%-20% chance that they'll need to make some adjustment to their income.

Modelling retirement outcomes

It's a challenge for financial planners and providers to illustrate the inherent risk in retirement planning to clients. It's a common approach to use some form of deterministic projection. This is a straight-line projection with a static assumption for investment returns, inflation and longevity.

An Independent Review of Retirement Income[32] commissioned by the Labour Party and published in March 2016 by the Pension Institute's Professor David Blake and Dr Debbie Harrison has some key recommendations on the use of deterministic projections. Specifically, the report recommends that:

- the use of deterministic projections of the returns on products should be banned

- they should be replaced with stochastic projections that take into account important real-world issues, such as sequence-of-returns risk, inflation, and transactions costs in dynamic investment strategies

- there should be a commonly agreed parameterisation for the stochastic projection model used, ie a standard model should be developed

---

32 Blake, David P., Independent Review of Retirement Income: Consultation (March 1, 2016). Independent Review of Retirement Income, 2016. Available at SSRN: https://ssrn.com/abstract=2753689

MODELLING RETIREMENT OUTCOMES

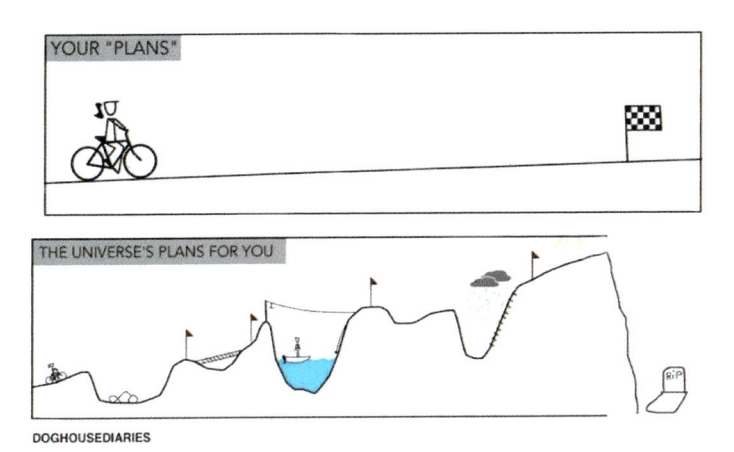

- there should be a commonly agreed set of good practice principles for modelling the outcomes from retirement income products

I don't personally support an outright ban on using straight-line projections, but I see strong reasons to rethink how we use them. I want to examine the strengths and weaknesses of the models financial planning uses, particularly in the area of retirement income.

Let's be clear. I truly believe in the role advisers play to help clients navigate the challenges of retirement income planning. But if advisers use models that lack empirical rigour, they do themselves and their clients a great disservice. These models fail to help clients understand the inherent risks in their plan and to prepare adequately.

After all, financial planning is a bit like a battle plan. No plan survives contact with the enemy. We need to be able to model scenarios, explore hidden risks and prepare accordingly.

Straight-line cash flow model

This is the simplest and most commonly used model by financial planners. A straight-line projection assumes the key variables of any financial plan (such as investment returns, inflation and longevity) are static.

Typical assumptions are often based on historical averages:

- investment returns = 5%pa
- inflation = 3%pa
- life expectancy = 90 years old

In straight-line projections, volatility doesn't exist, and investment losses are rare. Some planners build investment losses into specific years (eg, a 20% loss in year two and 15% loss in year six of the plan). But the rest of the periods are based on fixed, constant return assumptions (eg 3%pa).

There are two main problems with this. First, it bears no resemblance to reality. Investment returns have never behaved this way. And they most likely never will. By their very nature, investment returns and inflation are stochastic – which means that they are non-linear and largely unpredictable.

The second problem is that it inhibits planning by limiting the number of scenarios explored to one, or at best, a handful.

Clients end up with little or no idea about what kinds of market conditions could ruin their plans and what they might have to do to salvage the plan under those circumstances.

Milton Friedman once told us, *'never try to walk across a river just because it has an average depth of four feet.'* Sadly, this is what we do when we use straight-line projections in retirement income planning.

The weaknesses of straight-line projections in financial planning are well recognised and documented by early planners.

In 1994, financial planner Larry Bierwith noted the weaknesses of straight-line projections in an article[33] in the Journal of Financial Planning. He wrote, *'Traditional retirement planning ledgers create various scenarios of the future for a client by projecting constant rates of return and inflation over hypothetical future years. However, this approach can create a false sense of security for the client. Investment returns and inflation are never constant over time.'*

His article proposes an alternative approach: developing projections based on real historical data.

He noted that, *'By testing various investment approaches against historical data, the client can see the effects of varying rates of return*

---

33 Bierwith, Larry (1994). "Investing for Retirement: Using the Past to Model The Future." Journal of Financial Planning; Jan1994, Vol. 7 Issue 1, p14 https://www.onefpa.org/myFPA/journal/Documents/FPA%20Journal%20January%201994%20-%20INVESTING%20FOR%20RETIREMENT%20USING%20THE%20PAST%20TO%20MODEL%20THE%20FUTURE.pdf

and inflation through overlapping time periods, and the inevitable ups and downs of a portfolio over a typical retirement. By understanding the range of historical results, the client is better able to make informed investment policy decisions regarding the future.'

Bierwith's article prompted financial planner Bill Bengen to publish his first research that culminated in what is known today as safe withdrawal rate. In his article[34], Bengen noted, *'The logical fallacy that got our hypothetical planner into trouble was assuming that average returns and average inflation rates are a sound basis for computing how much a client can safely withdraw from a retirement fund over a long time.'*

The late financial planning legend Lynn Hopewell succinctly highlights why straight-line cash flow projections are grossly unfit for purpose when making financial decisions for unknown and unpredictable future events.

In an article[35] in the October 1997 edition of the Journal of Financial Planning he notes, *'In spite of the increasing improvement of financial planning software since the early 1980s, I know of no tools that explicitly deal with the uncertain nature of problem*

---

34 Bengen, William P. (October 1994). "Determining Withdrawal Rates Using Historical Data". Journal of Financial Planning: 14–24.

35 Hopewell, Lynn (1997). "Decision Making Under Conditions of Uncertainty: A Wakeup Call for the Financial Planning Profession." Journal of Financial Planning; Oct97, Vol. 10 Issue 5, p84 https://www.onefpa.org/myFPA/journal/Documents/Best%20of%2025%20Years%20Decision%20Making%20Under%20Conditions%20of%20Uncertainty%20A%20Wakeup%20Call%20for%20the%20Financial%20Planning%20Profession.pdf#search=Lynn%20Hopewell

variables. The tools are deterministic. No matter how well designed and how faithfully the software models a particular problem, it allows you to specify only one value for a variable. Yet, for real-world problems, the essential variables are uncertain; they can cover a wide range of values, and each value can have a different probability of occurring. Thus, stochastic tools are needed.'

It breaks my heart to think that in 2018, 20 years after Hopewell's first paper, not much has changed in terms of the primary model used in most financial planning software.

Historical scenario model

Historic market data offers us an interesting perspective on how investment markets work.

It's often said that past performance offers no guide to the future, particularly in relation to investment managers and funds. But if we look at asset class behaviour, this statement isn't entirely true. Extensive past performance going back over 200 years gives great insight into their behaviour. It doesn't tell us what the precise return might be next year, or in 10 or 20 years, but it offers an important perspective on the range of possible outcomes.

Why do we invest in equities, rather than keep money under the mattress over a very long term? Because equity past performance tells us that they'll most likely outperform cash over the long term. How do we know that equities tend to outperform bonds over the long term? Past performance tells us so. And of course, basic reasoning backs this up.

Renowned academics, from Harry Markowitz, Paul Samuelson and William Sharpe to Robert Shiller and Gene Fama, have greatly improved our understanding of how the capital markets work. In the process, they've won Nobel Prizes! Much of their work is based on the exploration of asset classes using extensive historical performance data. If it's good enough for Fama or Sharpe, it's good enough for me.

Financial planners can gain incredible insight by looking at how a financial plan would have fared under various real, past market scenarios. I am not talking about using a single historical market scenario or limited data based on a few years. That's almost as bad as a deterministic model. I am suggesting the idea of using sensitive historical data of 100 years or more, to gain colourful insight into how a plan fares under various scenarios.

Suppose we're working on a 30-year financial plan and we want to look at various scenarios over the last 115 years – how that plan fared in the periods between 1901 and 1930, 1902 and 1931 .... 1985 and 2014....1986 and 2015, and so on.

This gives at least 86 historical scenarios to look at. They include some of the most severe market conditions: two world wars, the Great Depression, periods of double-digit inflation, several recessions, booms and busts. We can see how the plan held up and what we could have done to prevent poor market conditions from ruining it.

There are a number of brilliant resources that provide extensive data for this sort of historical modelling.

- Morningstar DMS Database has been compiled by three brilliant professors: Elroy Dimson, Paul Marsh and Mike Staunton. It contains returns for equities, bonds, bills, inflation and currencies for 22 developed countries going back to 1900. A detailed explanation and summary data can be found in their book, *Triumph of the Optimists: 101 Years of Global Investment Returns.*

- Barclays Equity Gilt Study is a reliable source of data on long-term returns on UK equities, gilts, bills and inflation.

- Stocks, Bonds, Bills, and Inflation (SBBI) Yearbook is the industry standard performance data reference, with comprehensive records of US stocks, long-term government bonds, long-term corporate bonds, Treasury bills, and the Consumer Price Index dating back to 1926.

- Global Financial Data offers even more extensive data going back 200 years. The dataset includes annual and monthly returns of major asset classes, inflation and currency, as well as other important metrics such as bond yield, equity yields and PE ratios. https://www.globalfinancialdata.com/

- Bank of England: A millennium of macroeconomic data v3.1 (2016) was originally called Three Centuries of Macroeconomic Data, but has now been renamed to reflect its broader coverage. The dataset contains a broad set of macroeconomic and financial data for the UK, stretching back in some cases to the 13th century. (Credit: Thomas, R and Dimsdale, N (2017) "A Millennium of UK Data", Bank of England OBRA dataset.)

The main criticism of the historical model is that there simply aren't enough scenarios in history to account for the wide range of possible outcomes. Some periods overlap and aren't entirely independent of each other. Also, global markets are more complicated today than they've ever been and returns could be worse in the future.

As Peter Bernstein[36] eloquently highlights, this is an age-old argument. He notes that there's always been *'a persistent tension between those who assert that the best decisions are based on quantification and numbers, determined by the patterns of the past, and those who base their decisions on more subjective degrees of belief about the uncertain future. This is a controversy that has never been resolved. The issue boils down to one's view about the extent to which the past determines the future. We cannot quantify the future, because it is an unknown, but we have learned how to use numbers to scrutinize what happened in the past'*.

An article in the Economist[37] sums up why historical data, for all its faults, may be the most objective way to measure risk. *'When you use a financial model it requires assumptions about the underlying assets. These assumptions often are, but not limited to, the assets' expected price and volatility. Financial models find a price, and hedge against future fluctuations, based on these data points. There are two ways you can come up with these assumptions. You can use historical data or a personal view (from instinct, experience, or divine inspiration).*

---

36 Bernstein, Peter L.. Against the Gods: The Remarkable Story of Risk (Kindle Locations 241-248). Wiley. Kindle Edition.

37 Does the past predict the future? https://www.economist.com/blogs/freeexchange/2009/09/does_the_past_predict_the_futu

HISTORICAL SCENARIO MODEL

The problem with a personal view is that there always exists a temptation to use assumptions that make your product most attractive. When times are bad the market might question such optimism, but in the midst of a bubble few will (other than your boss who'll ask why your view makes less money than your rivals). Historical data, for all its faults, is the only objective way to measure risk.'

The author concludes, *'Historical data may be imperfect, but it remains the only unbiased way to measure risk and make assumptions about the future. Perhaps quantitative modellers in the future will reconsider what the appropriate length of history is. They may also test models more strenuously, forcing them to consider risk outside of historical bounds. Perhaps their managers will ask more questions about the implications of using particular data. Even these safeguards leave room for arbitrary decision-making. Still, during the next bubble, historical data will be the only thing that grounds finance in some reality.'*

Stochastic models

One way to overcome the weaknesses of a purely historical model is to use random simulations of historical averages or draw actual historical returns in a random order.

- **Bootstrapping:** this method involves randomly drawing actual historical monthly or annual returns to create likely future patterns of return. You're still using actual returns, but not necessarily in the order and combination that happened in the past. Bootstrap algorithms can be used to create as many scenarios as you want, using the actual behaviour of the asset classes involved.

- **Monte Carlo simulations:** Monte Carlo is a form of stochastic model that produces results based on repeated random sampling. The idea is to simulate thousands of possible market scenarios and identify a plan's probability of success or failure.

Monte Carlo modelling is a significant improvement on deterministic models. They take into account the unpredictability of returns, inflation and longevity. They're based on an assumed mean, standard deviation and correlation. They express potential outcomes in terms of the probability of successfully meeting clients' objectives.

This is a valuable aid to client communication. It gets clients and their advisers talking about financial planning

STOCHASTIC MODELS

and retirement outcomes in terms of probability rather than certainty. And this goes right to the heart of communicating and demonstrating clients' capacity for loss.

By its very nature, the future is unknown and unknowable. Monte Carlo simulations don't try to predict the future. In fact, it's the contrary. They generate thousands of possible future scenarios and identify what type of market conditions could ruin the client's plan. More importantly, this helps advisers and clients identify and agree what action they'd take if any of those nasty market scenarios happen. This to my mind is real financial planning.

One common criticism of a Monte Carlo model is that, given the low level of numeracy in the country, it might be hard to explain the results to clients. The joke is that 50% of the population don't understand probability and the other 50% have no idea what you're talking about.

Seriously, though, Monte Carlo is really easy to explain. I suggest that people think of the simulations as simply giving the client 10,000 lives (or 20,000 or whatever number of simulations you run). Each of those lives represents what your retirement could look like. We just don't know which one. We worry about the scenarios that result in the client running out of money and figure out what to do in advance.

You could use a simple, visual traffic light system to explain the success rate of a plan. Success rate of less than 60%

could be red, between 61% and 80% is amber and between 80% and 99% is green.

Monte Carlo simulations have their own weaknesses. The chief one is that returns in any one year are entirely independent of previous years. The implication is that Monte Carlo analysis tends to overstate tail risk, compared to the actual historical worst case. This is because Monte Carlo simulations don't account for mean reversion, which is a key characteristic of most asset classes.

As financial adviser and researcher Derek Tharp PhD notes: '*Whether the prior year was flat, saw a slight increase, or a raging bull market, Monte Carlo analysis assumes that the odds of a bear market decline the following year are exactly the same. And the odds of a subsequent decline in the following years also remains exactly the same, regardless of whether it would be the first or eighth consecutive year of a decline!*

Yet, a look at real-world market data reveals that this isn't really the case. Instead, market returns seem to exhibit at least two different trends. In the short-run, returns seem to exhibit "positive serial correlation" (ie, momentum – whereby short-term positive returns are more likely to be followed by positive returns, and vice-versa), and, in the long-run, returns seem to exhibit "negative serial correlation" (ie, mean reversion – whereby longer-term periods of low performance are followed by periods of higher performance, and vice-versa).'

So what?

My view is that both historical and Monte Carlo simulations are useful and certainly more robust than straight-line projections. Given that history represents past reality, many people, including me, give it more credence than most Monte Carlo simulations. Of course, it's possible that the worst years the stock market will ever see are in front of us.

If an adviser uses extensive historical data, they don't have to make assumptions about the behaviour of underlying asset classes. Historical data may only provide a limited sample of what's possible in the future, but the range of outcomes is wide enough to help us make informed decisions.

As Bernstein again noted, *'We all have to make decisions on the basis of limited data. One sip, even a sniff, of wine determines whether the whole bottle is drinkable. Courtship with a future spouse is shorter than the lifetime that lies ahead. A few drops of blood may evidence patterns of DNA that will either convict or acquit an accused murderer. Public-opinion pollsters interview 2,000 people to ascertain the entire nation's state of mind. The Dow Jones Industrial Average consists of just thirty stocks, but we use it to measure changes in trillions of dollars of wealth owned by millions of families and thousands of major financial institutions. George Bush needed just a few bites of broccoli to decide that that stuff was not for him. Most critical decisions would be impossible without sampling. By the time you have drunk a whole bottle of wine, it is a little late to announce that it is or is not drinkable. The* doctor cannot draw all your blood before deciding what medicine to prescribe or before checking out your DNA.'

Bernstein concludes that[38]:

'We cannot enter data about the future into the computer because such data are inaccessible to us. So we pour in data from the past to fuel the decision-making mechanisms created by our models, be they linear or nonlinear. But therein lies the logician's trap: past data from real life constitute a sequence of events rather than a set of independent observations, which is what the laws of probability demand. History provides us with only one sample of the economy and the capital markets, not with thousands of separate and randomly distributed numbers. Even though many economic and financial variables fall into distributions that approximate a bell curve, the picture is never perfect. Once again, resemblance to truth is not the same as truth. It is in those outliers and imperfections that the wildness lurks.'

---

38 Bernstein, Peter L. Against the Gods: The Remarkable Story of Risk (Kindle Locations 6827-6833). Wiley. Kindle Edition.

CHAPTER 8

Adapting sustainable withdrawal strategies to longevity

It takes two to tango but who's going to last longer, you or your portfolio?

So far, we've considered withdrawal strategies based on a fixed planning horizon. For consistency, we've used the 30-year retirement period but you can adapt all the approaches for any planning period.

The natural next step is to apply life expectancy, or more precisely longevity, into the sustainable withdrawal rate calculations. You can use mortality data available at the Office of National Statistics. Sustainable withdrawal rates should be based on survival probability, rather than a fixed (often longer) planning horizon.

Life expectancy: flawed measure for retirement income planning

Looking at life expectancy tables, based on the client's age and sex, is a common but flawed approach to estimating how long someone is likely to live. For instance, a 65-year-old man in the UK has a remaining life expectancy of 19 years, while it's 21 years for a woman of the same age.

This approach is flawed for several reasons. One, life expectancy is the mean number of remaining years. There's at least a 50% chance that someone in that age group will outlive their life expectancy! But more crucially, it fails to account for improvements in mortality as people get older.

The ONS has two types of life expectancy measure:

1. the period life expectancy which shows life expectancy at a given period eg for a 65-year-old in 2015

2. the cohort life expectancy which tracks a given cohort who share the same year of birth and takes account of improvements in mortality

The table below shows that mortality improvements add about three years to life expectancy for a 65-year-old male and female, depending on when they reach that age.

Cohort data is more appropriate for retirement planning purposes, because it takes into account likely future mortality improvement.

Year age 65 reached	2012		2037	
	Period	Cohort	Period	Cohort
Males	18.3	21.2	22.3	24.1
Females	20.7	23.9	24.7	26.7

Fig. 53: Cohort and period life expectancy for 65-year-old male and female. Source ONS, Dr Paul Cox[39]

---

39 See Paul Cox (2015): Helping consumers and providers manage defined contribution wealth in retirement. https://www.sanlam.co.uk/Sanlam/media/Retirement-Income-Service/Paul_Cox_Report.pdf This is an excellent discussion and essential reading on longevity assumptions in retirement planning.

Using survival probability

An obvious way to manage longevity is to use an annuity to ensure against the risk of living too long. Short of that, longevity in the context of retirement planning is best approached in terms of survival probability. This gives us a clearer idea of the chances that someone will live to a certain age.

The ONS cohort data in the chart below shows the survival probability for a 65-year-old male and female.

There's an 11% chance a 65-year-old male will celebrate his 100th birthday, and that rises to 15% for a female of the same age. For a couple of the same age, the probability that at least one of them will live to age 100 is a whopping 24%!

We need to bring the survival probability context into retirement income planning. This is one reason I believe that straight-line cash flow projections are inadequate. The challenge we're dealing with is – by its very nature – uncertain and so probabilistic.

This data is based on the general population in the UK so it's broadly accurate. But we can improve accuracy by using ONS cohort data for each part of the country.

Advisers can adjust survival probability even further to take account of a client's lifestyle. It's unrealistic to assume that a 65-year-old who smokes 10 packs of cigarettes a week, with

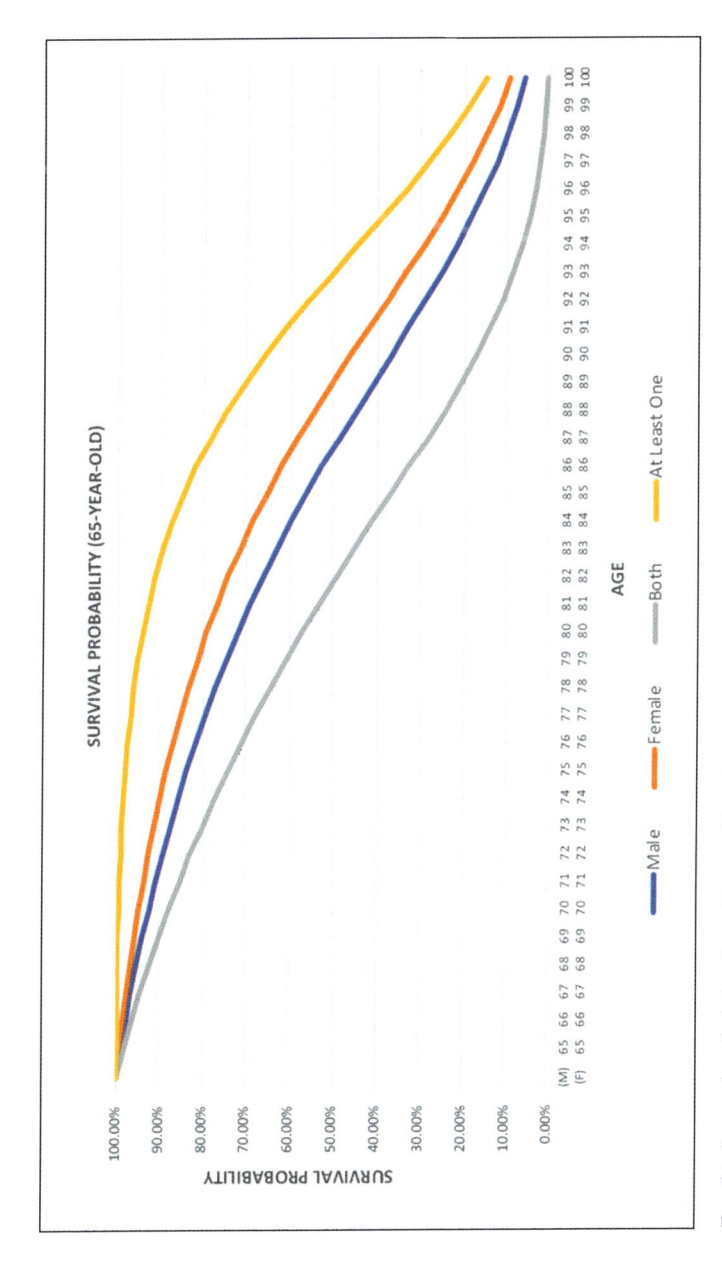

Fig. 54: Survival probability for a 65-year-old male, female or couple

mild health conditions, has the same survival probability as a health fanatic who goes to the gym three times a week and hasn't touched a cigarette in their life! Engaging in non-judgmental, grown-up discussions with clients is vital.

Longevity: human vs. portfolio

Once you've established the survival probability for an individual or a couple, you can estimate their probability of running out of money during their lifetime. The probability of success or failure should be based on how long the individual is likely to live, not a fixed period.[40]

To do this, there are two important factors at play:

1. the probability of failure of a withdrawal rate over any given fixed retirement period (eg 30 years)

2. the probability that at least one member of a couple will survive that period, given their current ages

These two factors are distinct and independent of each other – ie the chance of one happening doesn't depend on the other. (Although running out of money could well lead to an early grave.)

As these factors are completely independent, the probability of *both* happening is less than the probability of *either* of them happening. This is what maths nerds refer to as *conditional probability!*

---
40 See Stout, R. Gene and John B. Mitchell. 2006. "Dynamic Retirement Withdrawal Planning." Financial Services Review 15, 2 (Summer): 117–131

Earlier we said that a 3% inflation-adjusted withdrawal rate (net of 1%pa charges) from a 50/50 UK-centric portfolio has a 82.6% probability of success over a 30-year horizon. This means a 17.4% probability of failure. Or more precisely, a 17.4% chance that they'll need to make some adjustment to their withdrawal in the event of poor sequence of return.

But, for a 65-year-old couple, there's only a 48% chance that at least one of them will live to age 95.

The overall probability of running out of money during their lifetime is actually 8.4% (17.4% X 48%). So, the overall longevity-adjusted probability of success for a 3% inflation-adjusted withdrawal rate is a whopping 91.6%!

There are two unrelated probabilities here. So, for a client to run out of money, they need to experience both events at the same time – ie poor sequence of return that ruins a 3% withdrawal rate over a 30-year period AND at least one member of the couple surviving 30 years[41.]

---

[41] As you can see, the calculations are getting a bit more complicated. That's why a software tool is recommended for this – see www.timelineapp.co

Dealing with declining financial capacity in retirement

One final issue worth thinking about is that as people get older, their ability to make financial decisions is impaired. As discussed earlier, it's estimated that financial capability declines at a rate of 1% to 2% each year from age 60. So, expecting clients to understand the vagaries of managing a drawdown portfolio (or even to provide their adviser with informed consent to do so) is unrealistic.

One way to address this is to have a withdrawal policy statement[42] signed and pre-agreed by clients while they're still financially capable. Of course, clients over 65 should use Power of Attorney, particularly clients in drawdown. The attorney should be involved in the planning process as early as possible.

Longevity is a huge consideration in retirement, and it's an area where financial planning can add real value. The best approach to managing it is to use survival probability rather than putting a randomly selected age into the cash flow tool.

---

42 See 10.1 on the power of withdrawal policy statement

CHAPTER 9

Asset allocation and sustainable withdrawal rate

Asset allocation is a key factor when deciding the sustainable withdrawal rate from a retirement portfolio. Earlier versions of SWR research have been based primarily on domestic large-cap equity and bond portfolios. But an increasing body of study points to the vital role that broader diversification can play to improve retirement income sustainability.

Are you a stock or a bond?

One of the most important decisions a retiree must make is what proportion of their portfolio should be allocated to equities.

The received wisdom is that allocation to equities should be lower during the retirement income stage. Reasons include the fact that retirees tend to have lower risk appetites and reduced risk capacity.

Yet, this common industry practice isn't supported by cold, hard, empirical evidence. Indeed, in his seminal 1994 article, Bill Bengen recommended, '*a stock allocation as close to 75 percent as possible, and in no cases less than 50 percent. Stock allocations lower than 50 percent are counterproductive, in that they lower the amount of accumulated wealth as well as lowering the minimum portfolio longevity. Somewhere between 50-percent and 75-percent stocks will be a client's "comfort zone."*'

Other research, including mine, corroborates this view. Higher equity allocation tends to support higher sustainable withdrawal rates.

Fig. 55 overleaf shows the historical withdrawal rates for a 30-year retirement starting after 1900, using various asset allocations.

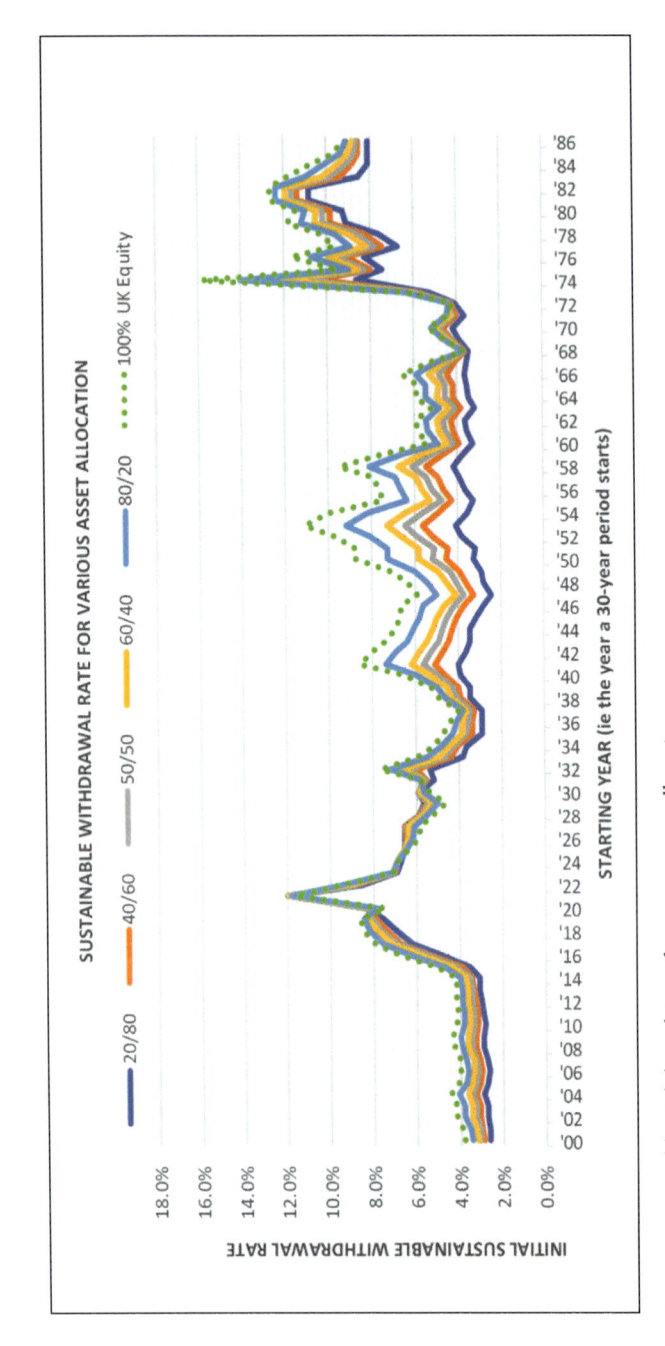

Fig. 55: Sustainable withdrawal rates for various asset allocation

ARE YOU A STOCK OR A BOND?

Fig. 55 shows higher equity allocation tends to support higher withdrawal rates. This is consistent through most historical periods.

Fig. 56 shows a summary of the historical worst case, 10th, 50th and 90th percentile net withdrawal rate (net of 1%pa fee) for varying degrees of allocation to equities, based on a 30-year horizon.

UK equity/UK bond percentage split	Historical worst case	10th percentile	50th percentile	90th percentile
20/80	2.5%	2.80%	3.7%	8.3%
40/60	2.9%	3.22%	4.5%	8.8%
50/50	3.1%	3.38%	4.9%	9.1%
60/40	3.2%	3.56%	5.3%	9.3%
80/20	3.5%	3.82%	5.9%	9.8%
100/0	3.6%	4.16%	6.3%	10.8%

Fig. 56: Gross withdrawal rates for various equity/bond allocations

Another way to view this is to look at the success rate of various asset allocations for a given withdrawal rate over multiple time periods. The chart below shows that higher equity allocations are consistently associated with a higher success rate over all time periods between one to 40 years.

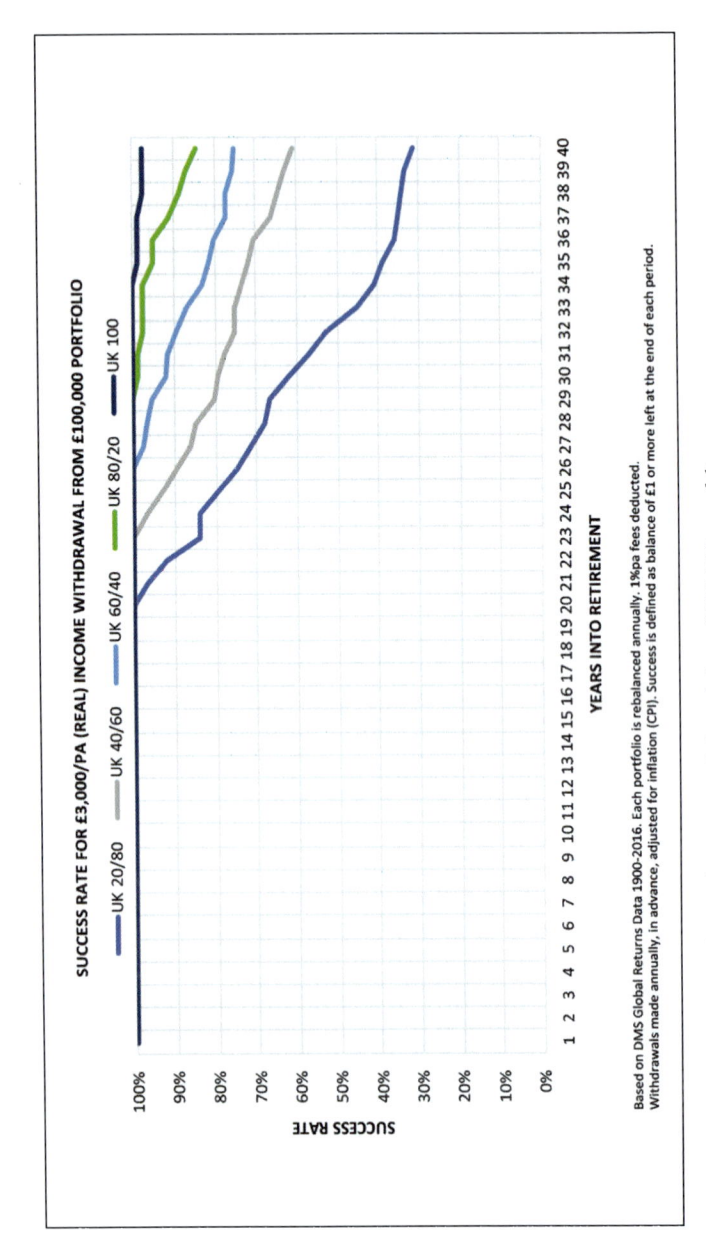

Fig. 57: Success rate for £3,000pa real income withdrawal from £100,000 portfolio

This raises an important question about how we assess risk in the context of meeting a retirement income goal. Why is higher equity allocation deemed to be higher risk, when it actually has a higher success rate?

The answer lies in the industry's misguided focus on volatility as the primary measure of risk. Higher allocation to equities is associated with higher volatility. In theory, this should matter less to the retiree, if the higher equity allocation gives them a greater chance of meeting their income objectives. But, in practice, investors contend with volatility on a daily basis. If the portfolio volatility is higher than the retiree is willing or able to accept, then there's a greater chance they might cave in and abandon the investment strategy.

The problem with high equity allocation in retirement isn't really an investment problem, it's an investor problem. Working with a financial adviser can be hugely beneficial here. An adviser can help reconcile the conflict between a client's willingness to tolerate volatility and the chances of meeting their income objective. A good adviser also provides an invaluable handholding service, particularly in extreme market conditions.

Ultimately, if retirees aren't prepared to accept at least 50% equity allocation, they'll need to accept a very low withdrawal rate or seriously consider a safety-first approach. In other words, annuitising some of their retirement funds to secure their income.

Small-cap and value equities

Is there a role for small-cap and value equities in a retirement portfolio?

Bengen explored the role of small-cap and value equities in research published in 1997[43], 2006[44], and then 2016[45].

His earlier articles noted that introducing small-cap and value equities into the portfolio mix significantly increased the SWR. But Bengen was cautious about the higher volatility associated with small-cap stocks and whether the outperformance of small-cap equities when compared large-cap equities (so called, small-cap premium) will persist.

When Bengen revisited the subject again in 2016[46], he was far more bullish about the improvement that small-cap and value equities added to the safe withdrawal rate.

---

43 Bengen, William P. "Asset Allocation for a Lifetime". Journal of Financial Planning, August 1996.

44 Bengen, William P. ("Conserving Client Portfolios During Retirement, Part IV". Journal of Financial Planning, May 2001.

45 Bengen, William P. (2006) "Baking a Withdrawal Plan 'Layer Cake' for Your Retirement Clients". Journal of Financial Planning, August 2006.

46 Bengen, William P, (2016) Small-Cap Withdrawal Magic. Financial Advisor Magazine http://www.fa-mag.com/news/small-cap-withdrawal-magic-28553.html

Bengen's findings were corroborated by Tomlinson[47] (2014) who considered the impact of small-cap and value stocks on withdrawal rates.

But does this hold up for UK retirees? I took a look at the impact of UK small-cap and UK value equities on withdrawal rate.

I constructed three portfolios:

- 50/50 UK small/bond portfolio
- 50/50 UK value /bond portfolio
- 25/25/50 UK small/UK value/bond portfolio

I compared the withdrawal rates over every 30-year period rolling since 1900 from these portfolios, to those of the baseline 50/50 UK equities/bond portfolio. You can see the results in the table below.

Fig. 58 shows that including value and/or small-cap in a retirement portfolio improved the sustainable withdrawal rate. Replacing all the equity allocation with value or small-cap improved the withdrawal rate for most of the time period. The median improvement is 0.4% for small-cap and 0.9% for value.

---

47 Tomlinson, J (2014) Do Small Cap-Value Stocks add Value in Retirement Portfolios? Advisor Perspectives. 4/8/14 by https://www.advisorperspectives.com/articles/2014/04/08/do-small-cap-value-stocks-add-value-in-retirement-portfolios

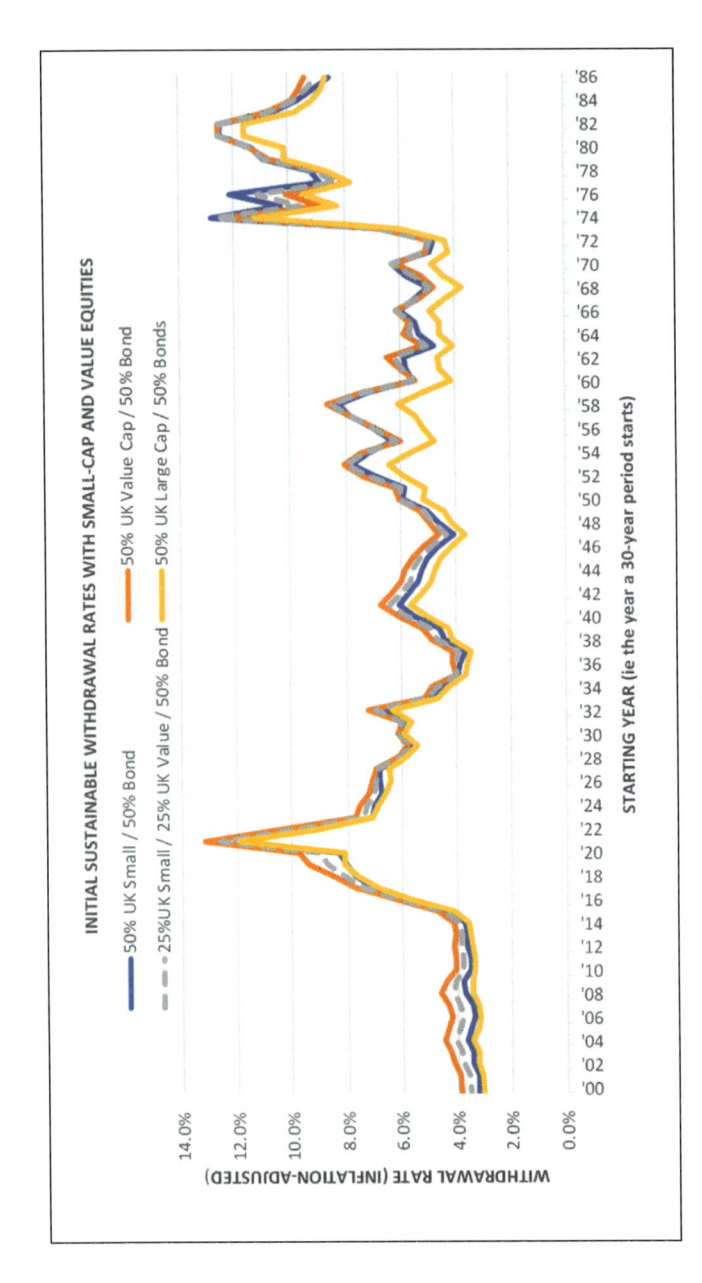

Fig. 58: Sustainable withdrawal rate with small-cap and value equities

SMALL-CAP AND VALUE EQUITIES

Fig. 59 below provides a summary of the withdrawal rates for each of the four portfolios, including the baseline portfolio.

	Worst	10th percentile	50th percentile	90th percentile
50% UK small-cap / 50% bond	3.2%	3.6%	5.8%	9.9%
50% UK value / 50% bond	3.8%	4.1%	6.0%	10.0%
25%UK small-cap / 25% UK value / 50% bond	3.5%	3.9%	6.0%	9.8%
50% UK large cap / 50% bonds (baseline)	3.1%	3.4%	4.9%	9.1%

Fig. 59: Percentile rate of sustainable withdrawal rate with small-cap and value equities

It shows that the gross withdrawal rate in the worst case is 3.1% for our baseline allocation, compared to 3.2% for small-cap, 3.8% for value and 3.5% for an equal blend of value and small.

Replacing large-cap equities with small-cap and value improved the sustainable withdrawal rate in virtually all rolling 30-year periods.

Fancy blending value and small-cap equities? No problem, you're in luck here too! Equally blending value and small-cap equities gives a withdrawal rate of 3.5%, an improvement of over 10% even in the worst-case scenario. Remarkably, we've achieved this uplift in withdrawal rate without increasing the overall equity allocation within the portfolio.

The positive results notwithstanding, I must sound a note of caution. A reason value and small-cap equities improved the withdrawal rate is simply because they deliver higher returns than the overall equity market.

Fig. 60 below summarises the annualised return, standard deviation, maximum gain and loss between 1900-2016.

	UK large-cap equities	UK small-cap equities	UK value equities
Average annual return	11.21%	13.66%	14.28%
Volatility	21.19%	23.40%	24.93%
Lowest annual return	-51.62%	-49.86%	-49.35%
Highest annual return	151.41%	117.25%	162.13%

Fig. 60: Annualised return, standard deviation, maximum gain and loss for large, small and value equities (1900-2015)

This dataset shows us that value and small equities do outperform, but with slightly higher volatility. They do seem to deliver higher risk-adjusted return though.

I'll leave the debate about exactly why value and small premium exists to financial academics. But there's extensive empirical research to show that value and small-cap premium does exist.

Dimson, Marsh and Staunton[48] addressed the question by noting that, '*The key question is whether the size premium will continue in the future. This is unanswerable since we cannot travel forward in time. However, we can at least travel farther back and look at virgin data for earlier decades, before 1955. As a result of the research for this book, we now have reliable UK stock returns data for the first half of the twentieth century, but unfortunately only for the largest one hundred stocks. This may nevertheless be enough to provide a pointer. Given that the size effect tends to operate across the entire size spectrum, if there were a size effect, we would expect to find evidence even among the biggest stocks.*'

They looked at the difference between equally weighted and capitalisation-weighted return of the top 100 stocks and concluded that this, '*provides some tentative evidence on the existence of a size effect over the first half of the twentieth century.*'

Dimson et al also attempted to answer the question of whether value premium existed pre-1956 and concluded that it did.

They noted that, '*Over the long term, the historical record of value investing has been positive in the United Kingdom as well as the United States. We now know that value stocks did better than growth stocks in the earlier as well as the later parts of the twentieth century. And the value-growth premium appears to be relatively robust to alternative definitions of value.*'

---

48 Dimson, Elroy; Marsh, Paul; Staunton, Mike. Triumph of the Optimists: 101 Years of Global Investment Returns (Page 127). Princeton University Press. Kindle Edition.

So, the key point is, including value and small-cap equities increases the SWR. The exact gain on withdrawal rate will depend on the intensity of the value and small-cap blend.

To go global or not? This is the question

One common question is around the impact of global diversification on SWR. We've known for some time that most investors exhibit a strong degree of home bias and allocate a higher proportion of their portfolio to their home market. But, the benefit of global diversification is generally accepted in the investment community.

So, what's the impact of global asset allocation on SWR?

Pfau 2014[49] conducted perhaps the most extensive study on the impact of global diversification on SWR. He calculated the local currency returns on stocks and bonds in 20 different nations for the same global portfolio. The portfolio consisted of the 20 countries in the dataset. This allowed for 20 different perspectives on the role of international diversification. Previous studies on withdrawals rates with international diversification have only looked within the context of US-based investors. Pfau's studies looked at SWR from the perspective of retirees in 20 different countries, investing globally.

Pfau concluded that global diversification helps more often than not – although it doesn't provide a complete panacea for market risk in retirement.

---

49 Pfau (2014): Does International Diversification Improve Safe Withdrawal Rates? https://www.advisorperspectives.com/articles/2014/03/04/does-international-diversification-improve-safe-withdrawal-rates

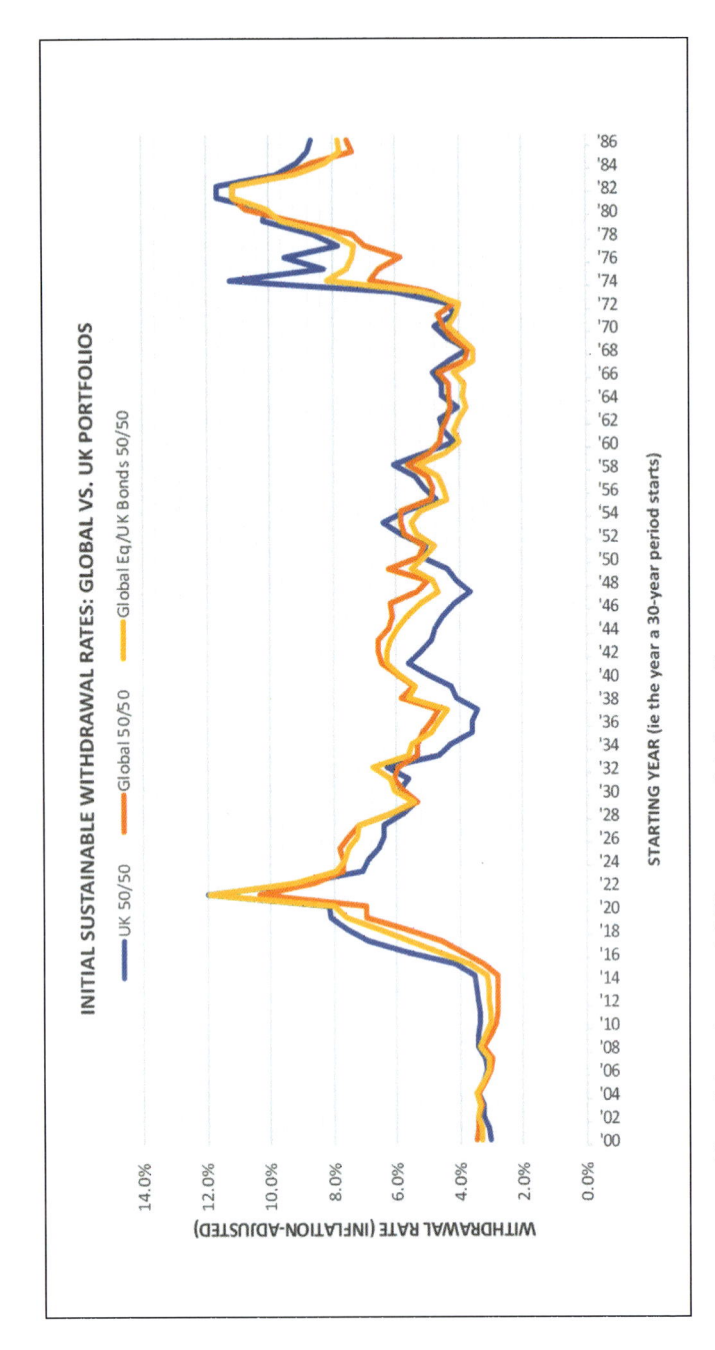

Fig. 61: Sustainable withdrawal rate with UK-centric vs. global asset allocation

TO GO GLOBAL OR NOT? THIS IS THE QUESTION

My research shows that a global asset allocation (ie 50/50 global equity/global bond split) results in a slightly lower sustainable withdrawal in 58% of historical periods when we compare it to a UK asset allocation. So, in 42% of historical periods between 1900 and 2016, global asset allocation results in higher SWR.

A closer look at the results reveals some particularly interesting patterns. Fig. 62 below shows the historical worst case, 10th, 50th and 90th percentile withdrawal rates for UK and global portfolios.

	Worst Case	10th Perc	50th Perc	90th Perc
UK 50/50	3.1%	3.39%	5.0%	9.1%
Global 50/50	2.8%	3.24%	5.3%	7.7%
Global eq/UK bonds 50/50	3.0%	3.28%	5.3%	8.0%
Global minus UK	(0.3%)	(0.2%)	0.4%	(1.3%)

Fig. 62: Sustainable withdrawal rate for global and UK-centric portfolios at various percentile rankings

In the worst-case scenarios, SWR for a global allocation is 0.3% lower than that of a UK-centric portfolio. This is because the SWR in these very bad scenarios is primarily due to the aggressive inflation during World War One. The average annualised inflation rate between 1914 and 1920 is 15.3%.

Because the main cause of a low SWR during this period was aggressive inflation, a global asset allocation did nothing to improve the SWR! Global equities returns were actually heavily weighted down by World War One, and fared worse than UK equities.

It's interesting that the median SWR is 0.4% higher for a global portfolio than a UK-centric portfolio. This suggests that in mild market conditions, a global portfolio produces a slightly better outcome. But, in extreme conditions - either very poor or very good sequence of returns - UK portfolios tend to support higher withdrawal rates.

Portfolios consisting of an equal split between global equities and UK bonds seem to fare slightly better than a global equities/bond portfolio. This is probably because UK bonds are a better hedge for UK inflation than global bonds!

Nonetheless, there's a strong case for global allocation in retirement portfolios. The annualised return on UK equity between 1900 and 2016 is 11.2%, with a volatility (standard deviation) of 21.2%. This compares to annualised return of 10.6% for global equity and a volatility of 16.26%. The lowest annual return on UK equity is -51.62%, compared to -31.4% for global equity.

	UK equity	UK bond	Global equity	Global bonds
Return	11.21%	6.19%	10.59%	6.56%
SD	21.19%	11.87%	16.26%	11.43%
Min	-51.62%	-17.39%	-31.36%	-17.06%
Max	151.41%	53.13%	54.10%	57.88%

Fig. 63: Performance of equities & bonds in £ (1900 -2016)

The UK equity portfolio may give a higher return, but it's also more volatile. For a retiree, a slightly lower SWR but with less volatility is probably preferable. That's what they get with the global allocation. They may sacrifice some upside and residual wealth, but they'll probably sleep more easily!

Commodities and alternatives

What about other asset classes?

Many people have questioned whether including other asset classes like commercial property and commodities improves withdrawal rates. We can't make an assertion one way or the other, because historical records for these asset classes don't go back far enough.

Cassaday (2006)[50] indicated that adding other asset classes, such as REITs, commodities and international exposures, potentially has a positive impact on sustainable withdrawal rates. However, this research was limited in its scope; the authors only used US historical data since 1972 and assumed 3% static inflation. So, the period covered in the research excluded some of the more severe periods like the early 1900s and 1936. It's not clear whether these asset classes would add much value under such stressful market conditions.

My take on this is that the likely benefit of adding these asset classes to a retirement portfolio are theoretical and at best, modest. These asset classes should only be used sparingly, if at all, (less than 10% of the portfolio allocation) and at very low cost.

---

50 Cassaday, Stephan (2006). "DIESEL: A System for Generating Cash Flow During Retirement", Journal of Financial Planning, September 2006

Impact of alpha on SWR

One common question about the SWR framework is what's the impact of superior investment return, also known as alpha, on sustainable withdrawals?

The logic goes that sustainable withdrawal rates are calculated using market returns (ie beta), so a retiree should be able to improve SWR by achieving higher risk-adjusted returns (ie alpha).

Alpha has the opposite effect that fees and charges have on sustainable withdrawal rate. A 1% improvement in risk-adjusted return over and above an index-based portfolio, results in a 0.5% improvement in withdrawal rate. Bengen (2006) framed this as the impact of the 'super investor' who generates portfolio alpha.

In practice, alpha is rare. If it does exist, it's a very shy animal. It's not like investment costs, which we know in advance and where we can see the impact. For all the energy spent chasing alpha, its relative impact on a successful retirement is minimal, compared with the impact of having a robust withdrawal strategy in place.

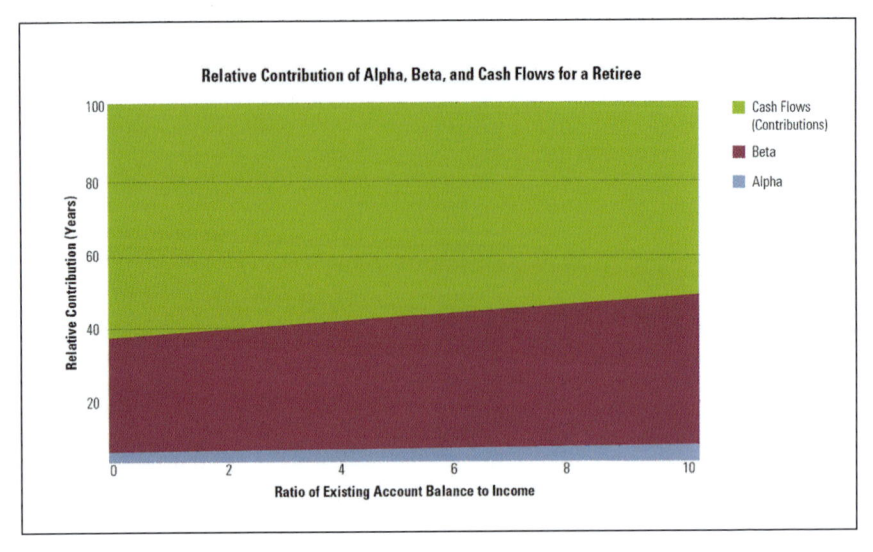

Fig. 64: Relative contribution of alpha, beta and cashflow (withdrawal rate) for a retiree

Research by Blanchett (2013)[51] considered the relative impact of alpha, beta and cashflow (ie withdrawal) on a retiree's overall outcome. The research notes that, *'while Alpha and Beta are important, a 1% change in the initial withdrawal rate (Cash Flow) has a greater impact than a 1% increase in return, either Beta or Alpha. Therefore, Cash Flows are the most important determinant of retirement success!'*

So, regardless of a retiree's wealth, market return (beta) and the withdrawal strategy (cashflow) explains over 90% of the success!

---

51 Blanchett, David M. 2013. "The ABCDs of Retirement Success." Journal of Financial Planning, vol. 26, no. 5 (June): 38-45

IMPACT OF ALPHA ON SWR

There are two ways to approach this from a SWR point of view.

- Ignore the impact of alpha when you calculate the initial sustainable withdrawal rate. You can increase withdrawal if alpha is delivered within the first few years of retirement.

- Take a higher initial withdrawal rate based on estimated alpha. Reduce the withdrawal rate if no alpha is delivered in the first few years of retirement.

It's best to ignore the impact of alpha when you calculate initial withdrawal rates. If you use rules-based spending methods, like Guyton's guardrail or Kitces' ratcheting, withdrawal will naturally be adjusted upwards if alpha is delivered in the first five years of retirement.

What low bond yield means for sustainable withdrawal rates

There have been concerns – voiced by several leading retirement income experts – that the era of low interest rates and low bond yields makes the SWR framework unlikely to hold up. Their argument is based on evidence that current bond yields are a strong predictor of future bond returns. Bond yields are currently low, so this suggests low returns in the next 10 years. And since the first decade of retirement largely predicts the sustainable withdrawal rate over the entire 30-year retirement, this implies a lower sustainable withdrawal rate.

We should take these warnings seriously. But it's important to remember that the SWR framework is based on expectations of low return in the first place.

While current bond yield is a strong predictor of future nominal bond return, it's a poor predictor of real (inflation-adjusted) bond return. Using data between 1900 and 2016, the coefficient of determination (R^2) between current bond yield and real bond return over the subsequent 10 years is 25%! This means that there is a lot about future real bond return that is not predicted by current bond yield.

We often hear that the so-called 'bond bubble' is about to burst. Some argue that this makes the sustainable with-

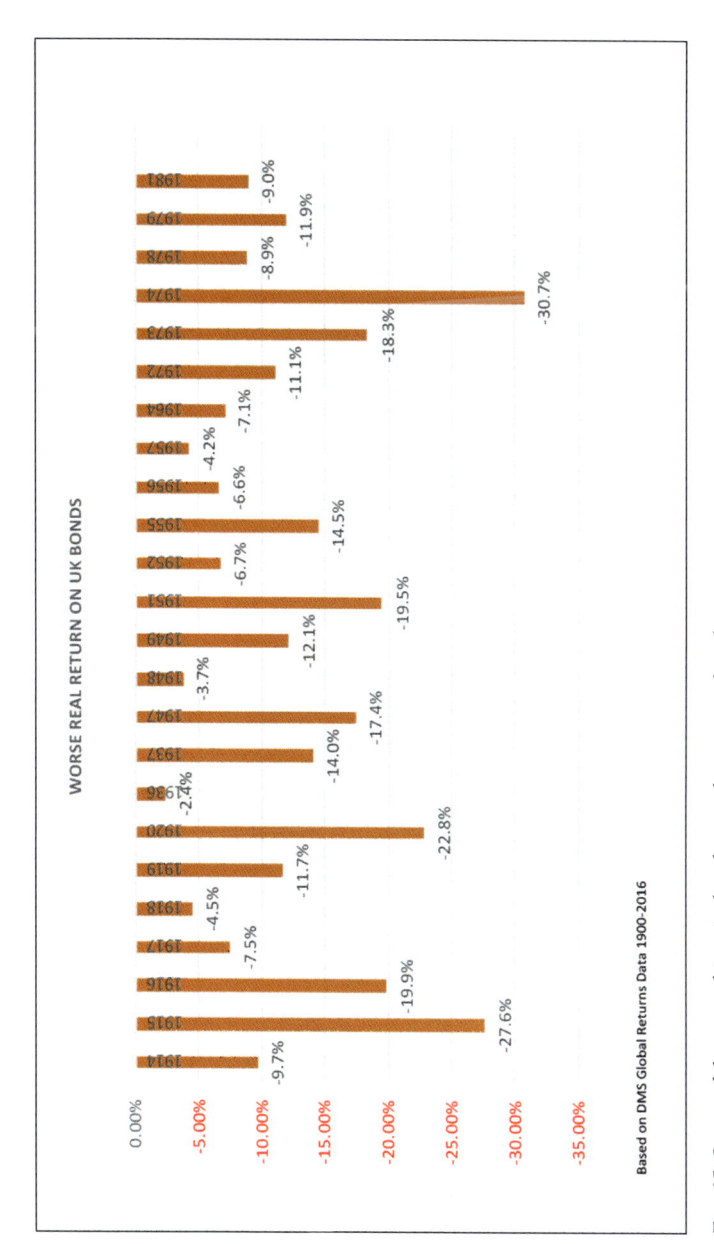

Fig. 65: Some of the worst historical real annual return on bonds

drawal rate framework unlikely to hold up in the future. But the real question is, is a downturn likely to be as bad as some of the worst bond returns in history?

The reality is that large losses on bonds are actually a fairly common occurrence. The SWR framework has survived periods of multiple negative double-digit bond returns. That's what it's been designed to do.

According to Professor Elroy Dimson, UK bond investors lost half their wealth in real terms in the inflationary period from 1972 to 1974! In the period between 1914 and 1920, UK bonds lost over 60% in real terms over seven consecutive years. But the SWR framework would have held its own during this period.

This is one important advantage of using extensive historical data to stress-test a withdrawal strategy. We can stress-test some of the most severe return environments and calibrate our plan accordingly.

What high equity valuation means for sustainable withdrawal rates

Another concern about the SWR framework is the likely impact of market valuation. Some of the concerns are valid, but many are misguided.

If we consider high equity valuations, they suggest lower-than-average expected return. But this is not necessarily the case.

The data available on UK equity valuation is somewhat limited, going back to 1926 for PE ratio and 1935 for Shiller PE10 (also known as the CAPE ratio). The data shows clearly that there is an inverse relationship between the PE ratio in a given year and the annualised real return on equities over the subsequent 10 years.

However, we should be extremely cautious if we use current equity valuations to predict future equity returns, in the medium to long term. Using UK data between 1926 and 2016, the R^2 between current PE ratio and subsequent 10 years' real return on UK equities is 20%. For Shiller PE10, the R^2 is 22.5%. In other words, the predictability of future return, using current PE or CAPE ratio, is lower than the flip of a coin.

Nonetheless, given current high equity valuation, future returns are likely to be lower than the historical average. Thank goodness, the SWR framework isn't based on historical average. It advocates a strategy that survives some of the most severe market conditions in history.

This highlights the need for flexible withdrawal strategies that will adjust withdrawals in the event of poor market conditions. Add to this a global asset allocation approach, rather than one that's heavily dependent on a single country.

CHAPTER 10

All together: baking the layer cake of sustainable withdrawal rate

So, we've considered the key factors that affect sustainable income in a retirement portfolio. Now the question is, how do we bring them together to construct a sustainable withdrawal strategy?

Bengen[52] (2006) suggests an approach similar to baking a cake. First, we determine the foundation layer (the main withdrawal strategy), then we decide which other layers we want to add.

Here's a list of the key factors that affect the layer cake:

1. foundation withdrawal strategy (inflation adjustment)
2. asset allocation (including small cap/value)
3. probability of success
4. fees

---

52 Bengen, William P. "Baking a Withdrawal Plan 'Layer Cake' for Your Retirement Clients". Journal of Financial Planning, August 2006

5. longevity adjustment
6. bequest
7. expected investment alpha

To illustrate this layer cake approach, I'm going to use a couple of scenarios. First, James and Janet Balance. Mr and Mrs Balance are both 65 and both drawing their State Pension. They're looking for a stable income from their £200,000 portfolio.

They talk to their financial adviser and agree to invest in a balanced portfolio. The Balances want to adjust their withdrawal with inflation each year and feel comfortable with a 90% probability of success. They're prepared to take less from their portfolio, but only if market conditions force them to. Of course, they have the house to fall back on if they need.

Their adviser bakes their withdrawal layer cake like this:

90% Probability of success (longevity adjusted)	+0.4%
Half of equity allocation (30%) invested in small cap/value	+0.5%
60/40 asset allocation (rather than 50/50)	+0.1%
Base withdrawal strategy: Bengen's constant inflation adjustment	3.1%
Fees (1% pa)	-0.5%

They end up with a sustainable withdrawal rate of 3.6% in the first year of retirement. This gives them an annual income of £7,200pa, based on their £200,000 portfolio.

ALL TOGETHER: BAKING THE LAYER CAKE OF SUSTAINABLE WITHDRAWAL RATE

Next, we meet Mr Cooks. He's 65, single and just started drawing his State Pension. His house is paid off and he has a portfolio of £300,000.

Cooks wants to enjoy his retirement while he can and intends to do a bit of travelling before winding down gradually. So, he quite likes the idea of being able to spend more early in his retirement and plans to spend progressively less as he gets older.

In terms of risk appetite, he's prepared to stomach some volatility. He agreed a 70/30 portfolio and an 80% probability of success with his adviser, after much discussion. He fully accepts that if he experiences poor market conditions in the early stage of his retirement, he might have to curtail his travels a bit. But that's a risk he's prepared to accept.

His financial planner bakes his withdrawal layer cake like this:

No request goal	0%
80% Probability of success (longevity adjusted)	+0.7%
Half of equity allocation invested in small cap/value	+0.25%
70/30 asset allocation (rather than 50/50)	+0.3%
Base withdrawal strategy: Guyton guardrail strategy	3.5%
Fees (1% pa)	-0.5%

This scenario results in an initial withdrawal rate of 4.25%. It gives him an annual income £12,750pa on top of his State Pension.

Withdrawal policy statement

Making sure a retirement portfolio lasts a lifetime is a bit like running an egg-and-spoon race.

Managing withdrawals is a delicate balancing act, thanks to the complex and nuanced nature of mitigating sequence and longevity risk. It's challenging for retirees to stay on track when they're making portfolio withdrawals – especially with markets throwing tantrums at the same time, like a toddler deprived of its toys.

We've already seen that managing a retirement portfolio involves making several complex decisions. They include:

- the baseline withdrawal strategy
- the withdrawal rates
- asset allocation and portfolio management strategy
- what proportion of portfolio (if any) to hold as a cash buffer
- in what order to liquidate asset classes and tax wrappers
- how to deal with one-off lump sum withdrawals over and above normal income needs

Often these decisions have to be made in client meetings and sometimes in the middle of a market tantrum. Most of these decisions and the trigger conditions have been pre-agreed, but they can still be unsettling and stressful for clients. At worst, clients can forget what's been agreed and they may have the impression that their planner is simply making things up as they go along.

Having a withdrawal policy statement (WPS) helps advisers and clients to have a pre-agreed framework in place to deal with these decisions. It's impossible for a planner to anticipate every possible market condition in advance. But, a WPS provides an anchor point for both clients and advisers when they're in the middle of a rapidly changing world.

Many planners have adopted an investment policy statement (IPS) as a set of guiding principles for decision making around asset allocation, re-balancing and discipline in the face of market turbulence. A WPS is a similar set of guiding principles around retirement portfolio withdrawals.

Financial planner Jonathan Guyton [53], one of the early proponents of the WPS, notes that, '*a withdrawal policy statement specifies the goals, policies, and parameters that the client and adviser agree to adopt to guide future decision-making regarding the use of the client's financial capital to help fund their lifestyle during their retirement years.*'

Guyton lists the essential components of a WPS as:

---

53 Guyton J (2010): The Withdrawal Policy Statement. Journal of Financial Planning, June 2010.

1. the client income goals
2. the client assets the WPS applies to
3. the initial withdrawal rate
4. the method for determining the source of each year's withdrawal income from the portfolio
5. the method for determining the withdrawal amount in subsequent years, including the trigger points for adjustments (other than an inflation-based increase) and the size of the adjustment

I believe that everything that has an impact on the withdrawal strategy should be included in the WPS.

A good WPS isn't a financial plan or a suitability report. It's a set of guiding principles about how to manage a client's withdrawal in line with their income objectives. The policy should be broad enough to encompass unexpected events as they happen and specific enough so the planner is rarely in doubt about the action to take when things change.

Of course, it's possible to implement a withdrawal strategy without a WPS. But because many of the strategies can have a direct impact on a client's lifestyle – such as freezing withdrawals (rather than increasing in line with inflation) or even a slight reduction in the withdrawal in extreme market conditions – having the client agree the WPS makes the process a lot more manageable. Crucially, it helps to avoid the impression that the adviser is making things up as they go along.

For instance, a client could agree a plan to:

- withdraw £10,000pa from a starting portfolio of £250,000
- increase the withdrawal amount with inflation each year, unless the previous year's portfolio total return was negative and meant the current withdrawal rate is bigger than the starting withdrawal rate
- reduce spending by 10%, if the current withdrawal rate is more than 20% above the starting withdrawal rate (eg if the starting rate was 5%, then the threshold is 6%)

The plan sounds reasonable, but clients will forget about it as they get on with their daily lives. And that's what you'd expect – it's why they hired an adviser in the first place. But when market conditions dictate that withdrawals have to be frozen or even cut by 10%, clients may not take too kindly to that idea if there isn't a written withdrawal policy statement. The opposite is also true. Clients could be unnecessarily anxious about normal market volatility if they don't have a written withdrawal policy statement.

Final words

Retirement income planning is one of the biggest financial challenges of the 21st century. It also presents an incredible opportunity for advisers to help clients navigate a complicated and potentially treacherous landscape at a crucial stage of their lives. However, this opportunity brings significant responsibility.

Given the enormous risks involved, retirement income planning should be viewed as a specialist area of its own. Advisers should only apply practices that are based on the best empirical and rigorous evidence available. If they don't, it'll mean poor outcomes for clients and eventually, for advisers.

Retirement planning is akin to mountaineering in many ways. Accumulation is the ascent and the decumulation stage is the descent. Financial planners are like mountain guides – financial Sherpas if you like.

Any mountain guide worth their salt will tell you that the skills needed to reach the summit are quite different to those for getting back down. They'll help you understand the risks associated with both legs of the journey and do their best to help you avoid them.

Take the earth's highest mountain, Mount Everest. Reaching its 8,848m summit is an achievement of epic proportions. But we don't often hear about the fatalities. There are no official records, but it's believed that around 280 climbers have died on Everest compared to around 4,000 climbers who've reached the summit.

Research in the British Medical Journal[54] shows that most climbers who die on Mount Everest do so above 8000m, usually during the descent from the summit. According to mountain climbing expert Stewart Green[55], most deaths occur while descending the upper slope, after they've reached the summit. It's in the area above 8,000m called the 'Death Zone.' The high elevation and corresponding lack of oxygen coupled with extreme temperatures, weather and some dangerous icefalls, create a greater risk of death than on the ascent.

Reaching the summit of a mountain is an incredible achievement, but it's a halfway point. American mountaineer Ed Viesturs, who has climbed Mount Everest seven times, puts it rather succinctly, *'getting to the summit is optional; getting down is mandatory.'* The summit is also the point of maximum risk.

Thankfully, most climbers avoid the dangers thanks to the Sherpas they hire to help carry gear, install ropes, and break tracks.

---

54 Firth P G et all (2008) Mortality on Mount Everest, 1921-2006: BMJ 2008; 337 doi: http://dx.doi.org/10.1136/bmj.a2654 (Published 11 December 2008) :BMJ 2008;337:a2654

55 Death on Mount Everest: How Climbers Die on Mount Everest http://climbing.about.com/od/mountainclimbing/a/Death-On-Mount-Everest.htm

This is true for retirement income planning. As financial Sherpas, advisers owe it to their clients to understand the particular dangers associated with the 'descent' and employ the best strategies to help them get to base as safely as possible.

About the author

Abraham is the creator of Timelineapp.co, a web-based software that illustrates sustainable withdrawal strategies. It's used by financial firms in UK, US, Canada, Australia and other developed countries. He is the founder of investment and retirement research consultancy, FinalytiQ. He hosts the annual Science of Retirement Conference in London, the go-to event for investment professionals looking to gain in-depth research-based insight on retirement income planning.

He's recognised as one of the country's leading experts in retirement income and investment propositions. Abraham has authored several industry papers and delivered talks to the Financial Conduct Authority (FCA), Chartered Insurance Institute (CII), the Personal Finance Society (PFS), the Association of British Insurers (ABI) and several conferences across the country.

He holds a Master's degree from Coventry University and an alphabet soup of qualifications, including the Investment Management Certificate, Chartered Financial Planner, Certified Financial Planner (CFP) and Chartered Wealth Manager designations. He was one of five finalists for the Professional Adviser Personality of the Year Award 2015 along with the then Pensions Minister. But the award went to a more deserving winner, obviously!

Timeline

Timeline is the sustainable withdrawal rate software used by financial planners in the UK, US and other developed countries across the world. Timeline uses extensive empirical research, asset class returns, inflation and mortality data to assess how a retirement strategy might fare under various market conditions.

All the withdrawal strategies covered in this book can be modelled on Timeline. Financial planners can visualise how these sustainable withdrawal strategies align with a client's needs, and produce a personalised Withdrawal Policy Statement for each client in minutes.

For more: www.timelineapp.co

FinalytiQ

At FinalytiQ, our aim is to help our clients deliver better outcomes to end investors than they would without our help.

To paraphrase American writer Edward Abbey, financial services is a bit like a stew. If you don't stir it up every once in a while, then a layer of scum floats to the top. That's why at FinalytiQ, we like to stir things up every now and then. We pride ourselves in spreading sunlight on the darkest corners of the investment world.

We provide critical analysis, benchmarking and insight to advisers, providers, and asset managers. Our particular areas of expertise include retirement income, investment propositions and benchmarking products/providers.

We support advisory firms with high-quality research and due diligence to create robust investment propositions that deliver superior client outcomes in a compliant way. Through our market analysis, benchmarking and thought-leadership content, we help platforms and asset managers identify their distinct positioning in the marketplace and build propositions that are fit for purpose.

For more: www.finalytiq.co.uk

Printed in Great Britain
by Amazon